THE ESSENTIAL JESUS
YOUTH EDITION

BY DOUG FIELDS
\\\\\ BASED ON THE BOOK BY WHITNEY T. KUNIHOLM + SCRIPTURE UNION

Copyright ©2014 Whitney T. Kuniholm

All Rights Reserved. Except as permitted under the U.S. Copyright Act of 1976, no part of this publication may be reproduced, distributed, or transmitted in any form or by any means, or stored in a database or retrieval system, without prior written permission of the publisher.

Published by CrossSection
940 Calle Negocio #175
San Clemente, CA 92673
800-946-5983
crosssection.com

Scripture Taken from the Holy Bible, New International Version®, NIV®.
Copyright © 1973, 1978, 1984, 2011 by Biblica, Inc.™
(Unless otherwise noted.)

Book + Jacket design by CrossSection.com

Set in Gotham & Scala

First Edition: August 2014

Printed in the USA

ISBN 978-0-9899537-6-4

THIS BOOK IS DEDICATED TO ALL THE AMAZING YOUTH WORKERS WHO SPEND THEIR TIME AND ENERGY HELPING POINT TEENAGERS TO JESUS. THANK YOU FOR YOUR COMMITMENT TO YOUNG LIVES, DISCIPLESHIP, AND LIVING OUT YOUR FAITH IN FRONT OF A YOUNG AND IMPRESSIONABLE AUDIENCE. YOU ARE MY HEROES.

—DOUG FIELDS

CONTENTS

Start Here: Read This First 7

Who Is Jesus? 15
① ② ③ ④ ⑤

OLD TESTAMENT

The Need for a Savior 25
⑥ ⑦ ⑧ ⑨ ⑩

Previews of a Savior 33
⑪ ⑫ ⑬ ⑭ ⑮

Psalms about a Savior 41
⑯ ⑰ ⑱ ⑲ ⑳

Prophecies about a Savior 49
㉑ ㉒ ㉓ ㉔ ㉕

More Prophecies about a Savior 57
㉖ ㉗ ㉘ ㉙ ㉚

NEW TESTAMENT

The Birth of Jesus 67
㉛ ㉜ ㉝ ㉞ ㉟

The Beginning Ministry of Jesus 75
㊱ ㊲ ㊳ ㊴ ㊵

The Sermons of Jesus 83
㊶ ㊷ ㊸ ㊹ ㊺

The Parables of Jesus 91
㊻ ㊼ ㊽ ㊾ ㊿

More Parables of Jesus 99
(51) (52) (53) (54) (55)

The Miracles of Jesus — 107
(56) (57) (58) (59) (60)

More Miracles of Jesus — 115
(61) (62) (63) (64) (65)

The Prayers of Jesus — 123
(66) (67) (68) (69) (70)

The Hard Sayings of Jesus — 131
(71) (72) (73) (74) (75)

The Crucifixion of Jesus — 139
(76) (77) (78) (79) (80)

The Resurrection of Jesus — 147
(81) (82) (83) (84) (85)

The Early Church of Jesus — 155
(86) (87) (88) (89) (90)

The Second Coming of Jesus — 163
(91) (92) (93) (94) (95)

Who Is Jesus... to You? — 171
(96) (97) (98) (99) (100)

Author Bios — 179

START HERE:
READ THIS FIRST

WHAT THIS IS GOING TO DO FOR YOU!

We are so excited for the journey you're about to take. Whether it was your idea to pick up this book or you were encouraged by a parent or friend, it's a good choice! Way to go! Actually, it's a courageous choice to spend time reading and thinking about and discussing God's Word. It could be the choice that changes your life! Congratulations!

In the following pages you'll be invited into the incredible story of Jesus. It's our prayer that somewhere in this story you'll find out where your own story intersects with Jesus.

Jesus is amazing! Everywhere that Jesus went, he drew a crowd and amazed people. What made him so amazing? That's the journey we are inviting you on.

Whether you are new to the Bible or you've been reading it for years, you're about to discover 100 reading selections that will give you a great overview of the Bible's central message about Jesus.

WHAT'S THE DEAL WITH THE ESSENTIAL JESUS?

These 100 readings contain a carefully selected list of short Bible passages that will expose you to the story of Jesus from the beginning to the end of the Bible. There are 25 Old Testament passages that point to Jesus, and 75 passages from the New Testament that paint different images of Jesus. We've organized the readings into 20 sets (often around themes) of 5 readings each so that you can more easily discover what the Bible says about Jesus.

Are you wondering why we chose 100 and not 30 or 50 or even 10? Fair question. We believe this number creates an opportunity for you to dig deeper into God's Word and at the same time helps you develop a Bible reading habit that will benefit you for the rest of your life. There are no "rules" in how long it will take... just keep reading until you finish, and then you can celebrate your big accomplishment.

START HERE

TAKE THE ESSENTIAL JESUS CHALLENGE

We're calling this the "Essential Jesus Challenge" as a way to help you, your youth ministry, your friends, family, and even your entire church read through the 100 Scriptures together.

Join the challenge! You can do it. Actually, if the people in your church aren't part of the challenge, step up and challenge them to join too. What you're holding is the youth edition of *The Essential Jesus*, but there's also another version for the non-youth in your church that can be found at ScriptureUnionResources.com.

HOW TO GET THE MOST OUT OF THIS BOOK

Please know that there's no ONE WAY to use this book on your journey with Jesus. You have the freedom to do whatever you want... you choose the time and the schedule. Please feel free to do whatever works best for you. Nothing is dated so you can use it at any time of the year and you can read it in 100 days or 1000 days... again, it's flexible and it's all up to you. Here are some specific tips to help you get the most out of your time:

1. Each reading is flexible enough for you to spend a minimal amount of time with the daily reading or an hour or so digging-in and making this a more profound experience. You can go deeper by answering the questions and really thinking through the passage so that you can discover how it relates to your life. You control the amount of time you want to spend with each reading.

2. Before you read, select a place that's comfortable for you where you won't be easily distracted. In today's world, it is so easy to get sidetracked! If reading at the same time each day is helpful for developing a habit, go that route.

3. Be sure to pick up a copy of *The Essential Jesus Bible Reading Planner*, our popular punch-out card that helps you track your 100-day reading progress. It's a lot of fun to use and you can order it from ScriptureUnionResources.com. We also encourage you to use the check circles in the table of contents to help you track your reading.

4. Try to find at least one other person to take The Essential 100 Challenge with you (parent, friend, youth pastor). Our experience is that you're more willing to keep going when you know you're not on the journey alone.

5 For each reading, we encourage you to follow our simple guided structure: (1) Pray it, (2) Read it, (3) Think about it, (4) Try it, (5) Write it, and (6) Meditate on it. Once you learn these simple actions, you can use them anytime you read a Bible passage. Here's how it works:

- **PRAY IT:** Before you read, ask God to help you understand his Word. We've written out a sample prayer to get you started.

- **READ IT:** Read the Bible passage slowly and thoughtfully. If you have time, read it more than once (or even aloud)… make the time to "take it in."

- **THINK ABOUT IT:** We provide a basic question to get you thinking about what you just read. You can answer it in your mind, talk about it with a friend, or write your response in space provided.

- **TRY IT:** We want you to learn from God's Word and then do something connected to what you just read. Many followers of Jesus… uh, well, they don't follow. They read, puff up with knowledge, and stay comfortable. We want you to put your faith into action in very real ways. Knowledge that travels from your head to your heart will impact your day-to-day life. If you don't like our "try it" suggestions… that's okay, just try something else.

- **WRITE IT:** There's something powerful that can happen when you put your thoughts, ideas, questions, dreams and prayers down on paper. We're big fans of journaling and want to challenge you to write stuff down. So find a journal or notebook and keep it nearby.

- **MEDITATE:** Meditate is a fancy word for "reflect" or "ponder." The idea here is to take one Scripture and think about it a little more. If you have extra time, write the verse down somewhere and take it with you throughout the day.

6 Finally, discuss what you read. Talk over the readings with a friend, your family, or within your small group. Adding dialogue to your study will transform your devotion time into a powerful spiritual experience. **At the end of every 5 readings, we've given you some questions to get your discussion started.** Again, you don't have to use our questions if you have better ones that will create more significant dialogue.

GROUP DISCUSSION INSTRUCTIONS

When you gather, use your first meeting to answer some basic questions: who will lead or facilitate discussion, and what's the best time/place/frequency of your meetings? Get those answers and you're on your way!

When you meet, keep in mind the following principles:

- **BE PREPARED.** Encourage every member to read the passages for the week prior to the meeting.

- **ENCOURAGE DISCUSSION.** Consider allowing everyone to share one thing they learned from their reading. Use the questions we've provided as a starting point for the group discussion. Don't feel the pressure to answer all the questions! We've given you several to choose from and your small group time may not be enough to get through them all. No big deal! Encourage the group members to take some time to answer the other questions on their own. As you are sharing your thoughts, make it clear that everyone should have an opportunity to participate and be careful not to allow one person to dominate the conversation.

- **LEARN AND LIVE.** Share examples of how you've tried to live out what you've learned. That's when the Bible will really come alive to you and others in your group.

DON'T RACE THROUGH THIS BOOK; WORK THROUGH IT SLOWLY

We encourage you not to speed through these readings so you can say, "I finished!" Our goal is that you'll gain more knowledge and love for Jesus and be able to say, "I know Jesus better!" He is the "star" of the Bible's greatest story—Jesus. As you read through these essential 100 passages you'll be able to discover for yourself who Jesus is and what makes him so special.

Our prayer for you is that over the next few months, the Bible's greatest story of God's love shown in Jesus will come alive for you as never before. Please don't allow these 100 readings to be the end of your journey in the Bible. Let it become the beginning of a lifetime adventure of connecting with Jesus through the Bible, prayer, and discussion.

If you would like another resource like this one, you might consider *E100* (100 Essential readings covering the Old and New Testament) and you can get that at ScriptureUnionResources.com.

We're excited to hear about your spiritual growth!
Doug Fields & Whitney T. Kuniholm

www.dougfields.com & www.scriptureunion.org

OVERVIEW

WHO IS JESUS?

The most important questions in life don't have to do with curfew, dating, how far is too far, or what's for dinner. You know that and that's why you're wise enough to be holding this book.

There are a lot of great questions to ask about purpose—what am I supposed to do with my life? Questions of philosophy—if God is loving, why does pain/suffering exist? Questions of relationships—why are people so difficult to get along with? It's probably safe to assume you've asked these questions and you've got many more great ones waiting to be answered.

But, there's one question that is more significant than all the others—Who is Jesus? Why is this so important? Well, because Jesus claimed he was God. When he was walking around on earth, he claimed to be both God and human. Pretty wild, huh? He said he was the fulfillment of God's promised Messiah—the one and only Savior of the world. Now if that is actually true, then that's a really big deal and all our other questions ought to get in line behind the question of "Who is Jesus?"

So, was Jesus who he said he was?

We think the best way to find out if Jesus really is God is to explore the most complete source of information we have about him—the Bible. As you read through these 100 passages about Jesus, you'll quickly see Jesus is the main character of the storyline that runs through the Bible from beginning to end. Jesus is what the Bible is all about.

In the first five readings, we'll consider the thoughts of three people who were very close to Jesus: John and Peter, two of his closest followers (also known as disciples), and Paul, who had a fascinating encounter with Jesus while trying to hunt down and kill Jesus' followers. Each of these five readings describes Jesus in very general ways. Later in our journey, we'll get into more specifics about Jesus' life (which is fascinating!). But for now, let's start with the big picture.

So, whether you're reading this on your own or discussing it with a small group of others, my prayer is that you'll gain a deeper understanding of how much Jesus loves you.

IN THE BEGINNING WAS THE WORD… THE WORD IS JESUS

PRAY IT:
Jesus, as I begin this journey of reading Your Word and exploring Your ways, please help me to see who You really are.

READ IT:
John 1:1-18

THINK ABOUT IT:
Why do you think Jesus is referred to as the "true light"? What are some helpful and/or attractive elements of "light"?

TRY IT:
When you walk by and notice a light switch today, consider these words: "Jesus is my true light."

WRITE IT:
Before you finish, take a little time to write your thoughts, questions, concerns, and/or prayers here...

The other writers of the Gospels begin their books with practical details of Jesus' life—who his ancestors were (Matthew), how his ministry got started (Mark), and how he was born (Luke). In this reading, John jumps right in by calling Jesus "the Word"… an interesting title highlighting something very important: **Jesus was different than other humans**. Jesus is not simply just a great teacher, healer, celebrity, or leader. The essential truth about Jesus is that he was "God in the flesh"… "God on earth" (verse 14). If you want to know what God is like, simply look to Jesus. Why? Because the Word [Jesus] was God (verse 1).

MEDITATE:

JOHN 1:1
In the beginning was the Word, and the Word was with God, and the Word was God.

2 HUMBLE JESUS

PRAY IT:
Jesus, speak to me as I interact with Your Word. Help me to see what You would have me see... I don't want to miss anything that You'd have for me.

READ IT:
Philippians 2:1-11

THINK ABOUT IT:
How difficult is it for you to look toward the interests of others? Do you think it's even possible to have the same mindset as Jesus (verse 5)?

TRY IT:
Identify one person in your life who you could serve today. How might you serve this person in the spirit of humility? Why might humility be an important character quality?

WRITE IT:
Before you finish, take a little time to write your thoughts, questions, concerns, and/or prayers here...

The Apostle Paul (the author of Philippians) challenged Christians to be less selfish and more loving, compassionate, joyful, and united (verses 1-4). In this challenge, Paul gives one of the most amazing descriptions of Jesus in the entire Bible (verses 5-11). Let's consider what he wrote about Jesus:
- Jesus is God (verse 6).
- Jesus became a human being (verses 7-8a).
- Jesus humbled himself (verse 7).
- Jesus obeyed God (verse 8).
- Jesus was exalted by God (verse 9).
- Jesus will be acknowledged by everyone (verses 10-11).
- Jesus became obedient to death—even death on a cross (verse 8).

Remember reading John 1:1-18... we're not talking about an ordinary man.

MEDITATE:

PHILIPPIANS 1:8
God can testify how I long for all of you with the affection of Christ Jesus.

3 IT'S ALL ABOUT JESUS

PRAY IT:
Jesus, You are amazing! I commit to read Your Word and think about Your ways today. I open my mind and my heart to You. Speak to me and may my heart be ready to hear You.

READ IT:
Colossians 1:15-23

THINK ABOUT IT:
Make a list of all the things that "Jesus is" according to these verses. Which one from this list makes you think, "Hmmm"? And which one makes you think, "That's right!"?

TRY IT:
Somewhere on these pages, draw a picture of something that would remind you that Jesus is to be the head of the church (verse 18). This isn't art class—you're not being graded. Have fun with it!

WRITE IT:
What else would you like to know about God? Make a list. What answers does Jesus provide? Remember, Jesus is the visible expression of the invisible God (verse 15).

The book of Colossians was written to reduce some of the negative impact that false teachers were having on new believers. These teachers created confusing ways for people to relate to God. Their teaching sounded impressive, but the central focus of Jesus was missing. To this day, theology and solid teaching are important to the Christian faith, but if Jesus is not at the center of it all, the teachers have missed the point.

MEDITATE:

COLOSSIANS 1:15
The Son is the image of the invisible God, the firstborn over all creation.

4 LOOK-A-LIKE

PRAY IT:
Jesus, I have so much to learn about You and Your character and I'm so hungry to know You better and thirsty to experience Your love. My prayer is that during this time I will draw closer to You.

READ IT:
Hebrews 1:1-4

THINK ABOUT IT:
Why would God want us to know what he's like? Why might knowing the character of God be important?

TRY IT:
Ask someone this question: "What do you think God is like?" Just listen. Don't judge. If the person returns the question to you, simply say, "I think he's just like Jesus." See where the conversation goes from there.

WRITE IT:
How would you describe what God is like? Write it out here:

The writer of Hebrews helps us understand that if we want to know what God is like, we can simply look at Jesus. Jesus is the "exact representation" of God (verse 3). Ever wondered what God thinks of the world? Look at Jesus. Ever been curious about what God likes and dislikes? On a closer investigation of Jesus, you'll find out. Want to know what God thinks about you? Again, look at Jesus—see how he loves.

Although Jesus was human, he was no ordinary human. As you read about Jesus, you might consider God is saying to you, "This is who I am... I want you to know me."

MEDITATE:

HEBREWS 1:3
The Son is the radiance of God's glory and the exact representation of his being, sustaining all things by his powerful word. After he had provided purification for sins, he sat down at the right hand of the Majesty in heaven.

5 THE CHURCH

PRAY IT:
Jesus, what a wonderful thing it is to know that You love me. I'm so very grateful and I look forward to learning more about Your love for me.

READ IT:
1 Peter 2:4-10

THINK ABOUT IT:
How does Peter describe "followers of Jesus" in this passage?

TRY IT:
Find a smooth stone and put it in your room as a reminder of these verses—Jesus is the main stone of the church.

WRITE IT:
Think about how you typically use the term "church." Do you normally refer to the building you attend... or do you think of "church" as God's people? How might that impact the way you use that word?

Following Jesus makes you one part of a really big group called the Church (big "C"). To help describe the Church, Peter uses a picture of bricks and cement, but gives it a spiritual meaning—it's a "spiritual house" made up of Jesus and his followers. In other words, the Church isn't a building, it's a "gathering of people who belong to God" (verse 9). The important part to understand is that Jesus is the foundation of this house... he's the most important element to this gathering (verse 6).

MEDITATE:

1 PETER 2:5A
... You also, like living stones, are being built into a spiritual house.

DISCUSSION QUESTIONS:
WHO IS JESUS?

PURPOSE:
To have a general discussion about Jesus and review what we already know.

QUESTIONS

1. How do you think most people view Jesus?

2. How does the media—movies, plays, television, or novels—portray Jesus?

3. How and when did you first learn about Jesus?

4. How would you describe your view of Jesus today?

5. Does it matter what people believe about Jesus? Why?

6. Is Jesus different from the world's great religious leaders? If so, how?

7. Does it matter that Jesus is "God in the flesh"?

THE ESSENTIAL JESUS YOUTH EDITION

OLD TESTAMENT

OVERVIEW

THE NEED FOR A SAVIOR

The Bible clearly teaches that Jesus holds the title of "Savior of the World." But, why do we need to be saved? What problem is so great that God had to come to earth to solve?

It's an easy answer, but not a fun one. The problem is described in the tiny word "sin," which creates big issues for us. In the next five readings we'll look deeper into sin and why our sin requires a Savior. Specifically, the Savior by the name of Jesus.

We'll begin by reading the account of "the original sin," when Adam and Eve disobeyed God in the Garden of Eden. The idea of a talking snake might seem funny today, but the reality of Satan and evil is really not humorous. Sin is what traps us, imprisons our heart, and destroys people.

Then we'll see a classic example of how sin spreads from an individual to a group of people (specifically the Israelites) and the messiness that results when sin extends beyond "a couple" to many. We'll finish this section of readings by looking at a few examples of sin from the Psalms and the prophets. Just a warning: this gets kind of ugly and you'll see how sin triggers God's anger. Bottom line, God doesn't like sin.

Some people would prefer we skip the "sin-parts" of the Bible and focus on the positive themes instead, like peace and love and joy and clowns (are there clowns in the Bible?). Sorry! Unfortunately, we've got to stop to think deeply about the reality of sin and its impact. We're born into a sin-filled (sinful) world and it holds us prisoner. That's why we need a Savior to set us free.

Jesus came to fix our sin problem and save us from living life separated from him. Key word: "save." The Savior saves us. So, let's face the truth about sin so we can face the good news of Jesus.

As you read or talk about this in your small group, be sure to be thinking of your own sin and why you need a Savior.

6 SIN AND OUR NEED FOR A SAVIOR

PRAY IT:
God, You have given wise and good guidelines for living. Show me more of Your good ways today and help me to sense Your presence as I reflect on Your Word...

READ IT:
Genesis 3:1-24

THINK ABOUT IT:
In verse 6 we see the "thought" of disobeying God's command turn into the "action" of intentional disobedience. How fast can you move from a sinful "thought" to a sinful "action"?

TRY IT:
Ask a friend this week to hold you accountable in a specific area of your life where you most easily give in to temptation. Who is a person in your life who is safe to talk to about the sin that most tempts you? What a gift to have that type of friend!

WRITE IT:
How would you define sin? Why does sin require you to need a Savior?

Adam and Eve had the perfect life: no work, no worries, no problems, no smog, no pain. All they had to do was obey one simple rule. It seems so easy, but there's something about human nature that draws us to disobey God's rules (see Romans 7:7-25). Our sin has consequences, as we see in this passage: shame (verse 7), fear (verse 10), pain (verse 16), and death (verse 19). The worst consequence is a broken relationship with God (verse 23) which requires us to need a savior. Sin opens the door for Jesus to walk in as the hero and save us.

MEDITATE:

GENESIS 3:4
"You will not certainly die," the serpent said to the woman.

7 TALK ABOUT WILD!

PRAY IT:
Jesus, it seems as though I am always so close to sinful disobedience. As I read and reflect on Your Word, please give me insight into my own sinful ways.

READ IT:
Exodus 32:1–33:6

THINK ABOUT IT:
Put yourself in Aaron's place as a leader... Where did his leadership fall short? What might you have done if you were in his position?

TRY IT:
Moses led. Aaron failed to lead. Both of these men were spiritual leaders. Write a letter of thanks to someone who plays the role of spiritual leader to you. Why is this person so important to your spiritual growth?

WRITE IT:
There are several weird and bizarre elements within this story. Write down what seems unusual to you. Who is someone in your life you can turn to in order to ask Bible-related questions?

There is so much going on in today's Bible reading. In the midst of life getting out of control, we see a wonderful example of God's plan for dealing with our sin problem. We see incredible human leadership: Moses volunteering to take the punishment that the people deserved (Exodus 32:31-32) and making a request for "atonement" (satisfying the requirements to restore our relationship with God—see Exodus 32:30). Atonement is exactly what Jesus did on the cross thousands of years later.

MEDITATE:

EXODUS 32:33
The Lord replied to Moses, "Whoever has sinned against me I will blot out of my book..."

8 IT'S NOT JUST THE BAD ONES WHO SIN

PRAY IT:
Dear Jesus, please help me to understand more about my own sin issues as I read Your Word today...

READ IT:
Psalm 14:1-7

THINK ABOUT IT:
In the NIV translation, it reads: "All have turned away, all have become corrupt; there is no one who does good, not even one." This paints a pretty depressing picture. How do you think this verse connects with the verses that we've looked at the previous couple of days?

TRY IT:
Read this passage again and then paraphrase it in your own words (don't worry about being exact—that's the beauty of paraphrasing). Try to use as few words as possible so that it will be more memorable.

WRITE IT:
When I think about the fact that God looks down from heaven to see if there's anyone who seeks him, it makes me feel... [write your response]

It's not just the bad, mean, nasty, villain-type people who sin... it's EVERYONE. Think: "ALL!" David ends his psalm with a prayer for a savior. Thankfully, God answered that prayer when Jesus came to restore ALL people from being captive to their sin.

MEDITATE:

PSALM 14:2
The Lord looks down from heaven on all mankind to see if there are any who understand, any who seek God.

THE NEED FOR A SAVIOR

9 HE'S AGAINST IT

PRAY IT:
Lord God, I ask that You would strengthen my relationship with You and give me deeper insight into Your ways as I spend time reflecting on Your Word.

READ IT:
Isaiah 59:1-21

THINK ABOUT IT:
In the *New Living Translation*, Isaiah 59:12 reads: "For our sins are piled up before God and testify against us. Yes, we know what sinners we are." Why do you think it's important to know about your sin?

TRY IT:
What are two specific ways you might demonstrate with your life that you are against sin?

WRITE IT:
Re-read Isaiah 59:20 and write it in your own words. What do you think the prophet Isaiah was trying to communicate? Is this good news or depressing news to you?

Isaiah reminds us that God is against sin. Sin separates us from God (verse 2). Remember reading about the beginning of sin (Reading 6—Genesis 3:23-24)? By the time of Isaiah, people were even more distant from God. More time, more sin, more separation. Today, the distance has gotten so great that some people believe God never existed. It's not really a surprise that God is against sin, but what is surprising is that God has had a plan to save us from all sin (verses 20-21). The plan was to send a Redeemer (20)—Jesus—who could restore the broken relationship forever.

MEDITATE:

ISAIAH 59:12
For our offenses are many in your sight,
and our sins testify against us.
Our offenses are ever with us,
and we acknowledge our iniquities...

10 OVERWHELMING ANGER OR EXTREME LOVE?

PRAY IT:
Jesus, please help me slow my mind and heart down to hear Your still, small, silent voice. I desperately need to be still and know that You are God...

READ IT:
Amos 5:1-27

THINK ABOUT IT:
It's obvious that Amos was addressing the rebellion of the people of Israel. Why do you think it's so easy for God's people to get sidetracked and rebel... even today?

TRY IT:
Amos encouraged his readers to seek the Lord (verses 4 and 6). How might you do that this week (seek after God)? Be specific.

WRITE IT:
Make a list of what you read in this Scripture that God doesn't like. Do any of these surprise you?

Wow! God has some pretty strong words about sin: "I hate... I despise... I cannot stand... I will not accept... I will have no regard... I will not listen" (21-23). Bottom line: God hates sin with passion! It can be frightening to think of God being angry. But when you consider the depth of his hatred for sin, can you begin to fully appreciate the power of his love for you by sending his own Son? Jesus willingly died for the sins of the world, the sins that God hated so much. That's not anger; it's overwhelming love.

MEDITATE:

AMOS 5:14A
Seek good, not evil, that you may live. Then the Lord God Almighty will be with you, just as you say he is.

DISCUSSION QUESTIONS:
THE NEED FOR A SAVIOR

PURPOSE:
To review sin and our need for a Savior.

QUESTIONS

1. In your own words, how would you define "sin"?

2. Do you think the church and Christian people think too much about sin or not enough?

3. How does it make you feel to know that God hates sin? How does it make you feel that God solved the sin problem for us?

4. How do you deal with sin in your own life?

5. Have you ever felt like you need a Savior in your life? When and why?

6. Do you think it's possible to understand the good news of salvation without understanding the bad news about sin? Why or why not?

7. What would you say to a friend who doesn't think that he or she has a sin problem?

OVERVIEW

PREVIEWS OF A SAVIOR

Are you one of those who likes to get to the movies early so you can watch the "previews"? I'm sure you know, but in case you don't, "previews" are short promotions for an upcoming movie that are shown prior to a full-length movie. Usually the preview provides a quick taste of the movie by revealing some of the most exciting scenes. Oftentimes, when you've seen the preview, you have a good idea of what's coming when the movie is released.

In our next five readings, we'll take a look at some fascinating previews of some coming attractions found in the Bible. We'll read five Old Testament previews that later have connections to the New Testament—(1) the Passover, (2) manna in the wilderness, (3) Moses lifting up the serpent, (4) the Temple, and (5) Jonah in the great fish. As you'll soon see, each one of these "previews" provides us with a unique picture of the Savior (Jesus) who would appear hundreds of years later.

Most people know that Jesus dominates the New Testament writings, but if you look for him, Jesus is also all over the Old Testament!

Just like in movies, the preview doesn't give away everything... the same is true with the Old Testament previews. The picture isn't totally clear and complete, but there's definitely enough to see that Jesus was part of the plan from the very beginning.

You'll enjoy these readings as you dig deep into the Old Testament in search for Jesus. And, if you're talking about this as a small group, encourage one another as you grow closer to Jesus.

11 LAMB, BLOOD & PASSOVER

PRAY IT:
God, I want to see You clearly in the history of Your Word. You made significant moves so many years ago that I want to better understand today and see how those moves point to Jesus. Help me to understand your ways.

READ IT:
Exodus 12:1-30

THINK ABOUT IT:
This passage contains two connections to Jesus: (1) lamb, and (2) blood. Based on what you know of Jesus, what do you think is the significance of these connections?

TRY IT:
Next time you celebrate the Lord's Supper (Communion), pause to think of this event and its connection to the Passover.

WRITE IT:
The death of the firstborn is the 10th and final plague that God unleashes on the hardened heart of the Pharaoh. For your own better understanding, go back to Exodus 6:10-13 and read what God required of Moses. Then, scan Exodus 7:14—10:29 and write down the other 9 plagues that followed the Pharaoh's rejection of Moses' cry, "Let my people go."

Let's be honest, today's reading is a little gross! Okay, a lot gross! Killing animals, handling blood, sudden death—yikes! But, this is one of the most important passages in the Bible. The Passover represents a powerful display of God's power in the Old Testament and it serves as a symbol of the most significant event in the New Testament. The writers of the New Testament often described Jesus as a lamb: "the Lamb of God" (John 1:29), "lamb without blemish" (1 Peter 1:19), and "Lamb who was slain" (Revelation 5:12). The Passover Lamb was one of the first great previews of God's plan of salvation. Another key part of God's plan for salvation was blood—the blood shed on the cross by Jesus' death was payment for our sin (Hebrews 9:11-14; Romans 5:9).

MEDITATE:

EXODUS 12:23
When the Lord goes through the land to strike down the Egyptians, he will see the blood on the top and sides of the doorframe and will pass over that doorway, and he will not permit the destroyer to enter your houses and strike you down.

12 TRUE BREAD

PRAY IT:
God, there are times when I'm really hungry for some real truth and words of real significance. Like I feed myself with food, I ask that You feed me in a spiritual way. I hunger to know You deeply.

READ IT:
Exodus 16:1-35

THINK ABOUT IT:
The long journey through the desert caused the Israelites to have a meltdown over food. The word "grumble" is mentioned 7 times in the first 11 verses. When you face a real problem, does grumbling and complaining make things better for you?

TRY IT:
Pray for your meal today. Pause before you begin eating to think about God's ability to provide.

WRITE IT:
Make a list of all the ways that God provides for you and takes care of your real needs.

In today's Scripture reading is another sign pointing to Jesus the Savior. In the New Testament, when the religious leaders demanded a miracle, Jesus pointed to this passage. He said that just as Moses provided manna to meet the physical need of people, so he, Jesus, was the "true bread" who satisfied the ultimate need of all people—the need for a restored and eternal relationship with God.

MEDITATE:

EXODUS 16:10
While Aaron was speaking to the whole Israelite community, they looked toward the desert, and there was the glory of the Lord appearing in the cloud.

13 TOO MANY SNAKES!

PRAY IT:
God, once again I come to Your Word hungry for more meaning, life, and connection with you. Please, bless me with new insight and understanding today!

READ IT:
Numbers 21:4-9

THINK ABOUT IT:
When the Israelites looked at the bronze snake they were saved from the effects of the poison. Can you think of any ways that the bronze snake and the cross are connected? (If you need a little help, consider that Romans 6:23 reveals that the consequences of sin is death.)

TRY IT:
Find or make a cross that you can put somewhere in your bedroom. Position it in a place where you'll see it while laying in bed and let it remind you of Jesus, his sacrificial death, and his unbelievable love for you as you drift to sleep.

WRITE IT:
If you were to place a small notecard near your cross, what words would you write on it? If you want, re-write those words on a piece of paper and place it near the cross in your bedroom.

At first glance you might think, "What's the big deal? Weren't the Israelites just being negative"? Well, yes, and they were also challenging God (verse 5)—that's at the very heart of all sin. God's main purpose was to provide a way for the people to be saved from the effects of the poison. But, notice that God didn't make the snakes go away, any more than he always makes our problems go away. He can make problems go away, but he's more concerned about our salvation.

MEDITATE:

NUMBERS 21:4
They traveled from Mount Hor along the route to the Red Sea, to go around Edom. But the people grew impatient on the way...

14 THE NEW TEMPLE

PRAY IT:
Jesus, I want to sense Your presence in my life. Thank You for the promise to make Your home in my heart.

READ IT:
1 Kings 8:1-21

THINK ABOUT IT:
What do you think it means that your body is a temple and that the Spirit of God lives with you? (See 1 Corinthians 3:16.) Why is that important for your life today?

TRY IT:
Google "Bible Commentary on John 2:19" and take some time to research what Jesus meant when he boldly said, "Destroy this temple and I will raise it again in three days" (John 2:19). What do you think he meant and why is that important today?

WRITE IT:
Write these words on a 3" x 5" card and keep them with you this week: "I trust in the presence of God right here. I rely on the power of God right now."

This reading describes the "ribbon-cutting ceremony" (or the grand opening) for a magnificent new Temple that King Solomon built as a place of worship. People would go to the Temple to meet with God (1 Kings 8:11-13). Today, our lives are the Temple for the Holy Spirit (see 1 Corinthians 3:16) and we don't need to go anywhere to sense his presence.

MEDITATE:

1 KINGS 8:13
I have indeed built a magnificent temple for you, a place for you to dwell forever.

15 RUNNING ON EMPTY

PRAY IT:
Dear God, I want to believe that everything happens for a reason and learn to be more thankful for the plans that You have for me. I want to be more like You.

READ IT:
Jonah 1:1–4:11

THINK ABOUT IT:
Is there any area within your life where you feel like you are "running from God"? Why do you think you might be on the run?

TRY IT:
Write down the names of two people in your life who seem to be resistant to God. Commit to pray for them and express your love/care to them.

WRITE IT:
Write your answer to this statement, "I tend to run from God when I am..."

During Jesus' day, he was confronted by some doubting religious leaders who asked for proof that Jesus was God. Jesus answered them by referring to the story of Jonah (see Matthew 12:38-45). Jonah provided the proof they needed. How? Just as Jonah was entombed in the great fish for three days, so Jesus would be in the tomb three days after his crucifixion. And Jesus would rise again; just as the great fish gave up Jonah, the grave would not keep Jesus. He is the true Savior! Because Jesus is the true Savior, he knows everything about you. You can't keep your "secret sins" from God. Jonah was foolish enough to think he could run from God. But really, that running from God is no more foolish than trying to think we can "get away" with sin... God always knows.

MEDITATE:

JONAH 2:2A
He said: "In my distress I called to the Lord, and he answered me."

DISCUSSION QUESTIONS:
PREVIEWS OF A SAVIOR

PURPOSE:
To review what the Old Testament says about the Messiah and consider what that tells us about our relationship with God.

QUESTIONS

1. Which of the five Old Testament stories in this section taught you the most about Jesus? What did you learn?

2. Do you know any media—songs, television programs, or movies—that seem to conflict with the Bible? How do they go off track?

3. How would you respond to someone who seems to misunderstand the Bible? Would you correct him/her, talk about it, show tolerance, or...?

4. What do you think is the best way to teach Christian truth? With symbols, examples, teaching, preaching, or...?

5. Is there a difference between complaining to God and being angry with him?

6. Is it okay to be angry with God?

7. What would you say to a friend who seems to be running from God?

OVERVIEW

PSALMS ABOUT A SAVIOR

The Book of Psalms is one of the most-loved, and perhaps most-read sections in the entire Bible. It contains lots of prayers, poems, praises, and crying scenes from some amazing servants of God—people like David and Solomon and Moses.

One of the reasons the Psalms are so rich in meaning is that they continue to develop the storyline about Jesus. Some of the Psalms are even called "Messianic Psalms" because they contain "previews" of the coming Savior/Messiah.

To give us a good sense of these Messianic Psalms, in this section of readings we will look at five of the most popular ones. As you read, take notice of how often Jesus is quoted from the Psalms. You'll read about his future crucifixion and realize that the cross was no "accident." It was actually God's plan—even hundreds of years before it happened. Also, as you read these psalms, consider the fact that you're reading the same psalms that Jesus read as a child. Jesus studied and memorized the Old Testament as a child, teen, and young adult. It's weird to think about Jesus reading about his future before it even happened.

Okay! Get ready for some exciting stuff as you dig into the Psalms and learn about our Savior. If you're reading on your own—way to go! If you're hanging out with some friends talking about God's Word—it doesn't get any better than that! Enjoy!

[If you have the time, you may want to read all of the Messianic Psalms back-to-back to get the full impact of them pointing to Jesus. The specific Messianic Psalms are 2, 8, 16, 22, 24, 40, 41, 45, 69, 72, 89, 102, 110, and 118.]

16 THE CASE FOR CHRIST

PRAY IT:
Jesus, regardless of what others do, I desire to follow You. Help me to grow closer to You today and better understand how You work and who You really are.

READ IT:
Psalm 2:1-12

THINK ABOUT IT:
"Anointed One" is another term for Messiah. What does that term mean to you?

TRY IT:
Pray for some of the leaders in your community, in your state, and in your country. Pray that these leaders would seek out the wisdom of Jesus.

WRITE IT:
Re-write this Psalm in your own words.

With the knowledge we have from reading the New Testament, it's much easier to clearly see several phrases within this Psalm that point directly to Jesus. The psalm's description of a Father's approval of his Son (verse 7) are the same words God would say to Jesus (recorded in the New Testament). Plus, the name given to Jesus (Messiah) means "Anointed One," which is the very phrase used in this psalm (verse 2). Also, when Peter and John were being harassed for speaking highly about Jesus after his resurrection, they quoted this psalm (see Acts 4:23-31). So, many years before Jesus appeared, the Holy Spirit was already developing a fascinating case for the coming Messiah/Christ/Savior.

MEDITATE:

PSALM 2:6
I have installed my king on Zion, my holy mountain.

17 AT THE CROSS

PRAY IT:
Jesus, it's so hard for me to imagine what You went through on the cross. I have no words to describe accurately how I feel other than thank You, thank You, thank You! Help me to better understand the depth of Your love for me today.

READ IT:
Psalm 22:1-31

THINK ABOUT IT:
What struggle is the author of this psalm experiencing? Why do you think he is able to end with such positive and confident words?

TRY IT:
Has God come to your aid in times of trouble? If so, identify a few ways you know God is involved and present in the midst of pain. Hang on to those ways and be ready to share them with a friend. Most people are hurting somewhere.

WRITE IT:
Read Luke 23:26-43. Write down the similarities between David's suffering (in the Psalm) and the suffering that Jesus went through at the cross.

This Psalm relates to Jesus because it's a vivid description of what Jesus would experience at his crucifixion. In fact, it was this very psalm that Jesus quoted while he hung on the cross, "My God, my God, why have you forsaken me?" (see Mark 15:34). David, the writer of this Psalm, describes the strong feelings of someone in big trouble. In the midst of his pain, David remembers what God had done in the past... that memory gave him hope to trust God in the present (in the midst of pain).

MEDITATE:

PSALM 22:11
Do not be far from me,
for trouble is near and there is no one to help.

18 "I'M IN DEEP WATER!"

PRAY IT:
Jesus, please show me the right way to react when others make fun of me or mistreat me. Help me to treat them in the same way that You would treat them and help me understand why You love them so much.

READ IT:
Psalm 69:1-36

THINK ABOUT IT:
How do you normally pray when you've been hurt or wounded by others? Is it okay to pray and ask God to hurt them?

TRY IT:
Write out the name of a person who has hurt you. Now, take some time to pray for that person. Ask Jesus to give you a heart like his.

WRITE IT:
List all the words in this psalm that have to do with water. Circle the words that "feel" desperate and underline the words that "feel" hopeful.

The writer of this Psalm (David) is in big trouble (2,14) and he's begging for God's help. It's not clear what type of problem David had, but he understood that God is a source of help. It's worthy to notice David's process. First, he is honest about his mess (1-4). Second, he examines his own heart instead of blaming others (5-6). Third, he makes his requests known to God (13-18), and finally, he ends by taking time to praise God (30-36). This psalm was especially meaningful to Jesus. He quoted it when explaining why the world hated him and his followers (see John 15:25).

MEDITATE:

PSALM 69:29
But as for me, afflicted and in pain—may your salvation, God, protect me.

19 WHO'S TALKING?

PRAY IT:
Jesus, I know that You are ultimately in charge now, and eventually everyone will recognize Your authority and power. As I think about Your Word today, please give me the wisdom to learn more deeply of Your ways.

READ IT:
Psalm 110:1-7

THINK ABOUT IT:
This Psalm paints a picture of Jesus' eventual rule over everything. What do you think it will be like when Jesus is recognized by everyone as God/Savior/Lord?

TRY IT:
Today's action is to read another section of Scripture: Matthew 22:41-45.

WRITE IT:
Write out the connection you see between Psalm 110:1-7 and Matthew 22:41-45. Do you think there's any significant connection?

Probably the most significant thing about this Psalm is the way it points to the coming Messiah (Jesus). In the New Testament, Jesus quoted from these Old Testament verses to challenge the religious leaders who doubted he was the Son of God (Matthew 22:41-45). These religious leaders thought the Messiah would be a human leader (from the family-line of David), but Jesus used these verses to demonstrate that the Messiah would also be God.

MEDITATE:

PSALM 110:1B
Sit at my right hand until I make your enemies a footstool for your feet.

20 THE CORNERSTONE

PRAY IT:
Jesus, You are so worthy of praise! I ask that You change my heart as I read Your Word and think more deeply about Your ways.

READ IT:
Psalm 118:1-29

THINK ABOUT IT:
Several times in this passage the psalmist writes, "His love endures forever." Why might it be a good thing to repeat this statement?

TRY IT:
"The stone the builders rejected" refers to Jesus (see Acts 4:11). When you're outside today, pick up a stone and put it in your pocket to be reminded throughout the day that Jesus is the "cornerstone."

WRITE IT:
Make a list of ways God has helped you in your life.

This passage contains one of "the greatest hits" from the Psalms: "This is the day the Lord has made; let us rejoice and be glad in it." This specific verse has become the opening sentence for millions of worship services around the world. But, even more important than a Psalm of praise is the description of Jesus as "the stone." Jesus was the stone that the religious leaders had rejected (see verse 22), and was the cornerstone (or "key/important/vital" stone) of the Church. In the New Testament, Jesus quoted this verse at the end of the parable about the evil tenants (see Matthew 21:33-46). Peter also referred to this when he called Jesus "the living Stone" (1 Peter 2:4-7) after his resurrection. Jesus is the rock—the foundation of the Church. Is Jesus the foundation of your life?

MEDITATE:

PSALM 118:24
The Lord has done it this very day;
let us rejoice and be glad in it.

DISCUSSION QUESTIONS:
PSALMS ABOUT A SAVIOR

PURPOSE:
To reflect on themes in the Psalms that teach us about Jesus.

QUESTIONS
1. Which of the five psalms in this section spoke to you the most about Jesus? Why?

2. Why do you think Jesus read and memorized Scripture? Can you think of other times when his biblical knowledge helped him?

3. What motivates you the most to read the Bible? When has the Bible meant the most to you in your life? Why?

4. What are your biggest obstacles to regularly reading the Bible? How could you overcome them?

5. Many people find the Bible to be more meaningful when they are struggling in some area of their life. Why do you think that is so?

6. What can a follower of Jesus expect from God during difficult times? Why?

7. What convinces you that Jesus is who he says he is? How have the Psalms helped you?

OVERVIEW

PROPHECIES ABOUT A SAVIOR

You're getting fair warning... this next section of readings may mess with your mind. Really! Prophecy can be mind-blowing! So, what exactly is biblical prophecy? It's definitely not simple, but simply put, prophecy is about announcing God's truth. Over the years, prophets spoke forcefully about God's standards and how God's people were called to live.

Another form of prophecy involves announcing God's plan for the future (also called fore-telling). Many Old Testament prophets would warn God's people that their sin and their worship of other gods would eventually bring punishment.

What's essential to understand about biblical prophecy is that the words that were spoken were not simply words from a human, they were God's words. A prophet is one who spoke for God.

In the next five readings, you'll be made aware of the prophecy and prediction of a coming Messiah who would bring salvation to the earth. Obviously, we think that Messiah is Jesus. Many think that Jesus is simply a character in the New Testament, but as we've read in previous readings, the prophecy of Jesus begins all the way back at the beginning of Genesis. You'll also read a few of the specific predictions about this "Anointed One" (who again, is Jesus).

The goal of these readings is for you to see that Jesus perfectly fulfilled every prophecy about the upcoming Messiah. It will be clear, but it may still be mind-blowing. If you're reading on your own... take your time, don't rush it. Take notes and write down questions that don't make sense. If you're reading these as part of a group... pause when you have a question—don't go too fast. Make sure that you "get it" before moving on. Have fun!

21 CHOSEN PEOPLE

PRAY IT:
Jesus, I ask You to help me see the power and potential of family today as I think and reflect on You. I'm grateful that I'm part of Your family—thank You for loving me so deeply.

READ IT:
Genesis 12:1-9

THINK ABOUT IT:
What currently holds you back from following God with your entire life? In what area of your life might God be asking you to trust him more?

TRY IT:
Come up with one specific action that you can take to "bless" someone in your family today. Make it happen and be reminded of the value of family.

WRITE IT:
Abram would begin the family-line from which Jesus would descend. In what ways have you been blessed by those in your family who came before you? Make a list.

Abram had no idea what God had in mind when God said, "All peoples on earth will be blessed through you" (3). All Abram knew was that God said, "Go," and he was obedient to God and he went. It's amazing what God can accomplish through one person who is willing to trust and obey him. God's call to Abram was no random act. God was putting in motion an incredible plan to reverse the impact of sin and to give humans a way to connect with God once again. The Scripture you read today only gives a short summary of what God had in mind (verses 2-3). It would take thousands of years for his plan of salvation (Jesus) to fully unfold.

MEDITATE:

GENESIS 12:3
I will make you into a great nation, and I will bless you; I will make your name great, and you will be a blessing.

22. THE GOOD SHEPHERD

PRAY IT:
Jesus, please open my eyes to see You more clearly and appreciate more of what You've done for me. Help me to see that You are the Good Shepherd who is faithful and loving to me.

READ IT:
Jeremiah 23:1-8

THINK ABOUT IT:
Why do sheep need shepherds?

TRY IT:
Read John 10:1-18.

WRITE IT:
Make a list of how Jesus describes the various characteristics of himself as the "good shepherd."

Jeremiah was sent to confront Israel's sin and encourage them to turn back to God. The religious leaders ("shepherds" in verses 1-2) felt the pressure of Jeremiah's prophecy. They were involved in un-godly activities instead of caring for God's people. The good news is that these "bad shepherds" highlighted the need for a savior—the "Good Shepherd" (Jesus—see John 10:11-18). In other words, God was planning to step into the picture to re-establish the right relationship between us and God, the relationship that had been destroyed because of sin.

MEDITATE:

JEREMIAH 23:5
"The days are coming," declares the Lord, "when I will raise up for David a righteous Branch, a King who will reign wisely and do what is just and right in the land."

23 O LITTLE TOWN OF BETHLEHEM

PRAY IT:
God, it's amazing that You care so much about me... You love me so much that You deal with my sin... You planned so well in advance that You knew You'd come to earth as Jesus to bring me salvation. I am so grateful today as I approach Your Word!

READ IT:
Micah 5:1-5

THINK ABOUT IT:
Do you feel like you are at peace with God?

TRY IT:
Spend some extra time today thinking about God's love that was revealed to us in Jesus.

WRITE IT:
Summarize the 5 verses that you've just read in less than 20 words.

In just these few verses from Micah's book we learn important details about the coming Savior, all of which were fulfilled by Jesus. We learn about his roots. The Savior would come from the little town of Bethlehem. We also learn about his character. Micah says that the Savior's strength and magnificence won't be based on human ability but on "the name of the Lord his God." And the Savior won't just achieve a time of peace, "he will be their peace." Micah's prophecy was clearly about Jesus who made peace with God by his death on the cross. How great is God?

MEDITATE:

MICAH 5:5A
And he will be our peace.

24 THE HUMBLE KING

PRAY IT:
Jesus, You are so worthy of praise and honor and glory, but You didn't seek it out or try to gain favor and popularity when You walked on earth. You were a humble and loving servant. I have so much to learn from You! May I see You and Your ways more clearly today.

READ IT:
Zechariah 9:9-17

THINK ABOUT IT:
In the Old Testament there are many "pictures" of a coming Messiah, Savior, Leader, Ruler that point directly to Jesus. Could it be that there are "signs" happening today that point to and reveal God's power, but most people don't assign to God? Can you think of an example?

TRY IT:
Make an intentional attempt at humility today: volunteer to sit in the back, stop yourself from bragging, turn the attention on a friend instead of yourself, let someone in front of you in line, etc... How does it feel to take on that role of putting others before yourself?

WRITE IT:
Write out your definition of humility.

Many Old Testament prophets talked about positive pictures of a future king. They created questions like, "What kind of king would come?" The Israelites wanted a strong king—someone who would fight and rescue them. But King Zechariah described a different kind of future king—one who would be humble (9), one who would bring genuine peace throughout the world (10), and one who would bring a new kind of freedom (11). It's not difficult to see his words fulfilled in Jesus. Jesus was a humble servant. Jesus brought freedom—by dying on the cross and freeing people from their sins (see Ephesians 1:7). Jesus will bring peace—still to come again, Jesus will establish an everlasting peace for those who believe in him (1 Thessalonians 4:16-17).

MEDITATE:

ZECHARIAH 9:9B (NLT)
See, your king comes to you, righteous and victorious, lowly and riding on a donkey, on a colt, the foal of a donkey.

25. FUTURE CLUES

PRAY IT:

Jesus, please help me to hear Your voice as I read and reflect on this passage today. I want to see You more clearly.

READ IT:

Zechariah 12:1–13:9

THINK ABOUT IT:

Is pride always bad? How could you avoid becoming proud in ways you shouldn't? How could you make praise for God a bigger part of your day?

TRY IT:

Today's prophecy reading refers to a fountain for cleansing from sin. So, as a reminder of what you read today, whenever you wash your hands say, "Thank you, Jesus, for cleansing me from sin."

WRITE IT:

Write down any images or phrases you see in this passage that might bring the person and life of Jesus to your mind.

The prophetic books (like Zechariah and others that we've looked at in this section, Readings 21-25) often contain clues to significant events that happened in the future. This passage contains several of those "future clues." One is Zechariah's reference to "the one they have pierced" (see 13:10). In the New Testament, John connected this verse to Jesus' death on the cross. Another "future clue" is found in the poem about the shepherd and the sheep, which is a familiar theme in the New Testament. While some of these Old Testament books are difficult to understand, they often quote God directly ("This is the Word of the Lord..."; see 12:1). God spoke to the prophets and they wrote down his words (that's what the "Oracle" in 12:1 means). And when God speaks, it's good to pay attention. God was speaking back then, and he's speaking now.

MEDITATE:

ZECHARIAH 13:9D

I will say, "They are my people," and they will say,
"The Lord is our God."

DISCUSSION QUESTIONS:
PROPHECIES ABOUT A SAVIOR

PURPOSE:
To discuss the general topic of prophecy and look at the major prophecies about Jesus.

QUESTIONS

1. What is prophecy? Describe it in your own words.

2. Do you think there is one correct interpretation of the Bible?

3. How do you treat people who have a different understanding of the Bible than you do?

4. Which of the prophecies is the best evidence for you that Jesus was the Messiah? Why?

5. Some prophecies describe a "suffering" and "humble" Messiah and King. Does that fit what you know about Jesus?

6. Why might it matter that these prophecies were literally fulfilled by Jesus?

OVERVIEW

MORE PROPHECIES ABOUT A SAVIOR

When it comes to the Old Testament prophets, the "the big man on campus" is Isaiah. The book of Isaiah is the longest of all the prophetic books and is the most quoted in the New Testament. But the most significant thing about Isaiah is that his prophecy gives us the clearest information about the coming Messiah (Jesus), which is why we'll spend the next five readings pursuing what God said through this amazing prophet.

The clearest descriptions of the Messiah (Jesus) are found in what is called the four "Servant Songs" of Isaiah. Each song describes various parts of "the Servant of the Lord." Interestingly, in the New Testament this phrase (Servant of the Lord) refers both to the nation of Israel and to the coming Messiah.

In the New Testament we see that Jesus was obviously aware of Isaiah's writing and prophesies about him and he took the role of Servant of the Lord for himself.

Probably the most famous passage in the book of Isaiah is the one in which Isaiah describes the "suffering Servant" (52:13—53:12). It's amazing to think that God gave Isaiah the words to describe the crucifixion of Jesus in graphic detail hundreds of years before it ever happened. And when Jesus walked the earth, he frequently explained that his mission was to suffer. But, as clear as the prophesies seem to us now, very few people understood them back then: not the crowds, not the religious leaders, and—oddly enough—not even Jesus' own disciples.

It's hard to imagine that the God of the universe would send his own son to die for the sins of humanity, but that's exactly what he did. And that's exactly what Isaiah prophesied... almost 800 years before it happened!

As you read, may God's Word come alive in your heart and draw you closer to him as you engage in his plan for your life. If you're doing this as part of a group, make sure you take time to pray and thank God that part of his plan is connecting you with others who want to know more about Jesus.

26 GOD WITH US

PRAY IT:

Jesus, there are times when I'm reading Your Word and I'm not sure what I'm reading—and my head hurts trying to understand. I pray that You help me understand the simple truths You'd have for me today.

READ IT:

Isaiah 7:1-25

THINK ABOUT IT:

What does it mean to you that God actually lived on Earth in the person of Jesus?

TRY IT:

Google the meaning of your name. It's as simple as typing "meaning of my name [your name here]." Write it somewhere on this page. Do you think it's accurate to how you approach life? Thank God that he knows your name and that you're not limited by someone else's definition of you.

WRITE IT:

Write down the name "Immanuel" on an index card. On the back of the card write down "God with us" and leave it somewhere in your room that you will see it regularly. Every time you see it, switch it from front to back or back to front. Remind yourself that God is with you.

This passage contains one of the most well-known prophecies about the coming Messiah in the entire Old Testament. Isaiah says that a virgin will give birth to a son who will be called Immanuel, which literally means "God with us" (see verse 14). The New Testament makes clear this prophecy was fulfilled in the birth of Jesus (see Matthew 1:18-25) where God sent his own son to deliver all people from sin. When God became flesh/human (in Jesus) the greatest miracle ever invaded human history—God is with us!

MEDITATE:

ISAIAH 7:14

Therefore, the Lord himself will give you the sign: The virgin will conceive and give birth to a son, and will call him Immanuel.

27 HOPE FOR THE FUTURE

PRAY IT:
As I pause to read Your Word and reflect on Your love, I ask for insight into Your ways. I want to know them better so I can better follow You, Jesus.

READ IT:
Isaiah 9:1-8

THINK ABOUT IT:
How have some of the more painful circumstances in your life drawn you closer to God?

TRY IT:
Whenever you turn on a light switch today, say to yourself, "Jesus is a great light for me." (See Isaiah 9:2.)

WRITE IT:
Write out these four names from today's passage: (1) Wonderful Counselor, (2) Mighty God, (3) Everlasting Father, (4) Prince of Peace. Next to each name, write out how you think Jesus fulfills that title.

God was planning a future for his people that would be wonderful in at least three ways: (1) Light. God would turn the darkness into light (see verse 2) through their eventual rescue from the Assyrian army. (2) Joy. This rescue would lead to a wild joy (verse 3). (3) The Coming Messiah. This future would conclude in the birth of one who would become a unique leader (verses 6-7), the promised Messiah. This prophecy was fulfilled in Jesus, who delivered us from the darkness of sin into the light of his presence.

MEDITATE:

ISAIAH 9:6B
And he will be called Wonderful Counselor, Mighty God, Everlasting Father, Prince of Peace.

28 THE CHOSEN SERVANT

PRAY IT:
Jesus, as I read this passage today, my prayer is that You will move my heart closer to You.

READ IT:
Isaiah 42:1-9

THINK ABOUT IT:
What is this servant to be like and what will he do? How can someone so quiet and gentle do these amazing things?

TRY IT:
Re-read verse 5 and then take some extended time to speak prayers of thanksgiving. What are you thankful to God for?

WRITE IT:
Verse 1 says that God "delights" in the chosen one (NIV). Another translation reads, "He is my chosen one, who pleases me" (NLT). Write down other synonyms for "delight" and "pleases" and re-read verse 1 using your chosen words.

This is the first of four "Servant Songs" in the book of Isaiah. God used this prophesy to communicate about the coming Messiah (Jesus). He has been chosen by God (verse 1). Isaiah prophesied that one day a Savior would come who would be uniquely chosen by God. He is God's instrument of salvation (verse 6). Isaiah says that the Servant would be filled with the Spirit of God (verse 1) and would establish justice for all (verse 4), including the weak and helpless. In the New Testament, Jesus would claim that he was the fulfillment of this passage (see Matthew 12:15-21).

MEDITATE:

ISAIAH 42:5
This is what God the Lord says—the Creator of the heavens, who stretches them out, who spreads out the earth with all that springs from it, who gives breath to its people, and life to those who walk on it...

29 THE SUFFERING SERVANT

PRAY IT:
Lord, I know that what I'm going to read today could have incredible impact on my life and I want to make sure I "get it"! Please give me a wisdom and insight that is so much deeper than my own so I may see Jesus more clearly.

READ IT:
Isaiah 52:13–53:12

THINK ABOUT IT:
What details about this unique servant did the Holy Spirit reveal to Isaiah?

TRY IT:
On Reading #13 you were challenged to either find or make a cross and then put it somewhere in your room where you'll see it often. Is it still there? Move it to a new location today so that it will feel new or different to you. As you see it, be reminded that Jesus suffered so that you might live—in eternity… but also today. The cross is a reminder that you can be fully alive today.

WRITE IT:
Today's passage reveals that *the servant's suffering would pay for the sins of others* (53:5-6, 12b). That's exactly what Jesus did on the cross. Write a short letter thanking Jesus for his sacrificial work on the cross.

In this well-known passage Isaiah introduces us to the "suffering servant" and in the process gives us a detailed picture of what Jesus would experience on the cross. What's amazing is that Isaiah wrote these verses about 800 years before Jesus lived! Isaiah couldn't have fully understood what he prophesied about; it even took Jesus' closest followers a long time to figure it out (see 1 Peter 2:21-25). Thankfully, we have the great advantage of seeing the full picture of God's plan of salvation.

MEDITATE:

ISAIAH 53:2
He grew up before him like a tender shoot,
    and like a root out of dry ground.
He had no beauty or majesty to attract us to him,
    nothing in his appearance that we should desire him.

30 MISSION STATEMENT

PRAY IT:
Jesus, may the light of Your Word shine into me to today so that it can be reflected toward all those around me. I want to be different because of You, Your love, and Your presence! As I read about Your character, help me see what You've called me to do and be.

READ IT:
Isaiah 61:1-11

THINK ABOUT IT:
What "mission" was this person "anointed" by God to accomplish? (See verse 1.) What might this mission tell you about God?

TRY IT:
Ask your spiritual mentor (someone you look up to) if he/she has a life mission statement. Keep asking those you respect until you discover someone who has one. Ask him/her how that life mission statement is used in his/her life.

WRITE IT:
How might you describe the mission statement for your life? If you can, take a few minutes to write it down.

This passage had special significance for Jesus; he used it as the mission statement for his life on earth. Near the beginning of his public ministry, Jesus stood and read this passage in the Temple, boldly claiming that he had fulfilled its words (see Luke 4:14-21). Jesus understood that he came to offer God's forgiveness and hope to those held prisoner to sin and to bring God's justice to those who were poor and abused. That's an amazing mission... and it's good news!

MEDITATE:

ISAIAH 61:1B
He has sent me to bind up the brokenhearted, to proclaim freedom for the captives and release from darkness for the prisoners...

DISCUSSION QUESTIONS:
MORE PROPHECIES ABOUT A SAVIOR

PURPOSE:
To discuss how prophecies about Jesus' life and ministry relate to our lives.

QUESTIONS

1. Which of these prophecies seemed to you to be the best proof that Jesus was the Messiah? Why?

2. Which of the names for Jesus is the most special to you? Why?

3. Have you ever felt that God has abandoned you? When? Do you ever feel that God is with you? When?

4. What tempts you to give up hope for the future? What gives you hope for the future?

5. Jesus said he came to bring good news to the poor, the prisoners, the blind, and the oppressed. Is it realistic for you to do the same? Why?

6. Why did Jesus have to go through such incredible suffering?

7. What does God's sacrifice of his Son tell us about God? Does it change how you value your life?

OVERVIEW

THE BIRTH OF JESUS

Alright everybody... the rest of our time reading will be spent in the New Testament. It begins with the birth of Jesus and goes past his death and resurrection. As you think of the birth of Jesus, you've got to think about the true meaning of Christmas. And that's exactly what our next five readings will help us better understand. We'll read the familiar story of Joseph and Mary making the journey to Bethlehem, of an unlikely birth in a manger, of the shepherds, the angels, and the heavenly hosts all welcoming this special child... Jesus.

The birth of Jesus was definitely not a random act! As you know from your previous readings in the Old Testament, God was clearly at work orchestrating everything behind the scenes. It's wild to think that the promised Messiah would be born to a young virgin... in a barn—not the stereotypical, grand entrance fit for the King of the World, right?

You'll also notice references to Old Testament prophecies. As we discovered in earlier readings, God had given many "previews" that he was planning to send a Savior to the world. The good news is that it was finally time for the main event and the Savior to appear. He entered the world in the person of Jesus.

Finally, it's fascinating to examine how all the different people in these next readings reacted to the birth of Jesus. Joseph and Mary, the shepherds and wise men, religious leaders and King Herod, all struggled with what was happening and the looming importance behind these events. Thousands of years later, we are able to more fully appreciate the truth as expressed in one of the names used to describe Jesus, Immanuel, which means, "God with us." That's what this next section is all about.

Enjoy your reading! Jesus is spectacular and you'll see why everyone was amazed. If you're reading this as part of a group, make sure you don't read so fast hoping to finish that you miss the awesomeness of God. Alright, dig in!

31 FAVOR WITH GOD

PRAY IT:
Jesus, there is so much to know and understand about You and Your ways... I want to know You better and more fully. I beg You to speak to me today through the power of Your Word.

READ IT:
Luke 1:26-56

THINK ABOUT IT:
How do you think you would respond if an angel appeared to you?

TRY IT:
Which of Mary's qualities do you see most in your life? Make a commitment to express one of those qualities today.

WRITE IT:
If you heard these words, "Greetings, you who are highly favored! The Lord is with you" (28), how would you feel? Write out your feelings.

The Bible indicates that Mary was "greatly troubled" (verse 29) and afraid (verse 30) when the angel appeared to her. But, she didn't run in fear; she stayed and listened—pretty amazing! Mary is one of the great heroes of the Bible who found favor with God. What can we learn from Mary's life? First, she is confident in her relationship to God. She sees herself simply as "the Lord's servant" (verse 38). Second, she expressed a willingness to live by faith (verses 38 & 45), something that is so rarely seen today. Finally, she had a heart for God (verses 46-55), which made her so attractive. Mary's song (verses 46-55... often called the *Magnificat*) is filled with Old Testament imagery and reveals that Mary was a young woman who had spent time reflecting on the Scriptures.

MEDITATE:

LUKE 1:30
But the angel said to her, "Do not be afraid, Mary; you have found favor with God."

32 — IMAGINE THE SURPRISE

PRAY IT:
Jesus, when You invaded earth as a human You changed everything! Now, please change me as I draw close to You through Your Word.

READ IT:
Matthew 1:18-25

THINK ABOUT IT:
Why is the obedience of Joseph so important to this story? The surprise he experienced had to be indescribable in that his whole world changed with one announcement—it's pretty wild to consider.

TRY IT:
Spend a few minutes thanking God for all the amazing details and events that went into the birth of Jesus.

WRITE IT:
Imagine that you are Joseph for a minute and you're about to write an opening statement to your very best friend about what you just experienced with the angel... How would you word this?

As we read in this passage and several others related to Jesus' birth, God sent angels to explain his intentions and to direct the action when necessary. Not only that, as we have already discovered in Readings 1-30, God arranges amazing details to bring about his plan. Speaking of amazing, how about the idea of the virgin birth (20)? After all, we know science and biology and acknowledge that a virgin birth could never happen, right? But just because something is beyond our understanding doesn't mean it couldn't be true. What is impossible to humans is possible to God.

MEDITATE:

MATTHEW 1:21
She will give birth to a son, and you are to give him the name Jesus, because he will save his people from their sins.

33 JESUS IS GOOD NEWS

PRAY IT:
Jesus, thank You for the people who shared Your good news with me. Their words and understanding of You have helped the depth of my faith. Help me understand more of You so I might be able to share Your good news with others.

READ IT:
Luke 2:1-40

THINK ABOUT IT:
Which character in Jesus' birth story do you most identify with? Why?

TRY IT:
The angels shared the "good news" with the shepherds. Try doing the same thing this week. Make a commitment to share the good news of Jesus with someone you care about.

WRITE IT:
Based on what you know about Jesus, write out a Top 10 (or 5) list of what makes Jesus good news.

Typically, the most overlooked characters in this passage would be the lowly shepherds. But, what makes this section of Scripture exciting is how they responded to the good news. The shepherds weren't too busy to investigate the claims about Jesus (verse 15). They made finding Jesus a high priority (verse 16), and they didn't consider the truth about Jesus "a private thing." Instead, they immediately began telling others what they had discovered (verse 17) and weren't embarrassed to enthusiastically worship God (verse 20).

The actions of the shepherds sure seem like good qualities to possess for those who follow Jesus today.

MEDITATE:

LUKE 2:17-18
When [the shepherds] had seen him, they spread the word concerning what had been told them about this child, and all who heard it were amazed at what the shepherds said to them.

34 ON THE MOVE

PRAY IT:

Jesus, I don't want to be someone who simply knows a lot about You and Your Word but never gets beyond mere head knowledge. Help me learn how to apply Your Word to my everyday life.

READ IT:

Matthew 2:1-23

THINK ABOUT IT:

Think of the most difficult situation you are currently facing. What is the real reason it's so difficult right now?

TRY IT:

Spend time asking God to show you what he is doing in your life. Sit quietly for a few minutes and simply listen. Ask God to help you trust that he'll take care of you.

WRITE IT:

This passage of Scripture has people searching for Jesus (Magi, Herod). One group finds him (Magi) and the other (Herod) doesn't. Make a list of what you've been searching for as a follower of Jesus (for example: hope, healing, acceptance, answers, etc...).

One unique feature of this passage is the journey of Joseph and Mary—they traveled a lot. Their son was the [promised] Messiah, so one would think their life would be safe and secure. But God's plan was for them to be a family-on-the-move. Today, being connected to Jesus isn't a commitment to safety. Following Jesus isn't "safe," but we can be confident that no matter where God leads, he has a purpose in mind (see Romans 8:28). With Mary and Joseph, God was protecting this special family and fulfilling the plan he had announced hundreds of years earlier. God always knows what he is doing in our lives, even when his plan doesn't appear clear to us.

MEDITATE:

MATTHEW 2:23

... And he went and lived in a town called Nazareth. So was fulfilled what was said through the prophets, that he would be called a Nazarene.

35 HIS FATHER'S HOUSE

PRAY IT:
Jesus, You are truly amazing! May I never lose my sense of amazement over Your love, Your teachings, and Your plan for my life. I want to be amazed by the power of Your Word today.

READ IT:
Luke 2:41-52

THINK ABOUT IT:
What do you think Jesus was like when he was your age?

TRY IT:
Make a list of some of the amazing statements and teachings of Jesus (you might want to write them down in the back of this book and keep adding to them as you read more about Jesus).

WRITE IT:
Come up with three answers to this statement: "Jesus, you're amazing because..."

As you read in this passage, Jesus possessed wisdom far beyond his years (47). At a young age Jesus already understood that he was God ("I had to be in my Father's house," 49). His claim of being God was not invented later in his life just so he could attract a crowd—Jesus was born fully human and fully God. The dialogue between Mary and Jesus also introduces us to a tension that builds throughout the Gospels. Jesus often said things that made it clear he knew who he was (God in human body). Some people were confused by what he said while others clearly understood him and just didn't like what they heard—they became angry and rejected him.

MEDITATE:

LUKE 2:52
And Jesus grew in wisdom and stature,
and in favor with God and man.

DISCUSSION QUESTIONS:
THE BIRTH OF JESUS

PURPOSE:
To review the major events surrounding the birth of Jesus as they relate to the way Christmas is celebrated today.

QUESTIONS

1. Throughout the account of Jesus' birth, God sends angels to announce good news and to direct the action. Why do you think he chose to do this?

2. When Jesus was born, the angel announced that it was good news. What exactly is the "good news"? Can you describe it in your own words?

3. Which qualities of Mary and Joseph appeal to you? Why?

4. Do you think most people know the real meaning of Christmas? How would you explain what Christmas is to a non-believing friend or family member?

5. Have you ever had an experience that made no sense at the time but later convinced you that God was at work? What happened?

6. Why do you think Jesus' claim to be the Son of God would make some people angry?

7. What facts about Jesus' birth are most meaningful to you? Do they affect the way you celebrate Christmas?

OVERVIEW

THE BEGINNING MINISTRY OF JESUS

In our next five readings, we'll see that Jesus goes from being an unknown carpenter to an incredibly popular preacher and healer. We'll begin by looking at Jesus' first public appearance where he's recognized as someone special. It was during the time when Jesus was baptized, by John the Baptist, that God announced, "This is my Son, whom I love; with him I am well pleased" (see Matthew 3:17).

From the very beginning it was clear that Jesus was more than a carpenter, and that's why the devil attacked him right away in the desert with different types of temptation (as you're about to read). How Jesus dealt with that temptation is incredibly helpful as an example to follow today—Jesus always returned to God's Word. You'll see, he would say, "It is written." There is power in God's Word and Jesus was making that very clear. Finally, we'll see Jesus explain his personal mission statement and then watch him begin to recruit others to become his closest followers.

One key theme that we'll see from these early days of Jesus' ministry is his commitment to finding followers. Throughout the Gospels we see Jesus presenting the simple challenge: "Follow me." That little phrase is packed with big meaning—both for his original audience and for those of us who follow him today (as you're about to find out).

These are some of my favorite readings. Buckle up, it's about to get pretty exciting! And if you're reading with some friends, be sure to talk about what it means to follow Jesus as a group.

36 THIS IS MY SON

PRAY IT:
Jesus, there are many things I don't understand but I desperately want to get closer to You. Please show me the areas within my life that keep me from drawing near to You.

READ IT:
Matthew 3:1-17

THINK ABOUT IT:
Which part of John the Baptist's message applies the most to you now: (1) to repent, or (2) that Jesus is near? Why?

TRY IT:
In verses 16-18, all three persons of the Trinity were involved: the Son was baptized, the Holy Spirit descended to Jesus, and the Father spoke. Read these 3 verses over and over and think about the powerful nature of God.

WRITE IT:
Write down the names of 3 friends and family members who could benefit from understanding the word "repent." Pray for an opportunity to share the truth behind John's message with them.

It appears as though John the Baptist was an odd character! But he had a powerful two-part message that people were hungry to hear. Part 1: "Repent!" (verse 1). John told people they were sinners and what they should do about it—turn from their sins (verse 8). You wouldn't think "repent" would be a popular theme, but when you're in prison to your own sin, a call to repentance (and being set free) can be life-giving. Part 2: "The kingdom of God is near!" This message had to do with Jesus and the fact that the Messiah was now with them calling them to live in a new kingdom.

MEDITATE:

MATTHEW 3:16-17
As soon as Jesus was baptized, he went up out of the water. At that moment heaven was opened, and he saw the Spirit of God descending like a dove and alighting on him. And a voice from heaven said, "This is my Son, whom I love; with him I am well pleased."

37 DELIVER US FROM EVIL

PRAY IT:
Jesus, I know there are many things in this world that bring me temptation and those things can easily separate me from You. Please give me the strength to fight off those temptations as I build my life on Your ways found in Your Word.

READ IT:
Luke 4:1-13

THINK ABOUT IT:
In which area of your life do you feel the most temptation (i.e. food, sex, money, power, etc...)?

TRY IT:
Be especially aware of temptations today. When you feel tempted, say what Jesus said, "It is written..." and then return to God's Word to be reminded of them.

WRITE IT:
Write out your strategy for resisting temptation (for example: prayer, talking to a friend, running from the situation, etc...).

In this passage, the devil attempts to destroy Jesus in three ways: (1) The promise of granting physical desires. The devil was trying to use Jesus' hunger to make him forget who he really was (God in a human body). (2) The promise of worldly power. The devil said, "If you worship me, it (all this) will all be yours" (verse 7). (3) The promise of spiritual power. The devil returns to his original taunt (verses 3, 9—"If you are the Son of God"). With each temptation, Jesus responds with these words, "For it is written..." Jesus met each of these temptations with the presence of Scripture, almost like a shield to defend himself from the devil's attack.

MEDITATE:

LUKE 4:4
Jesus answered, "It is written: 'Man shall not live on bread alone.'"

38 WHO DOES HE THINK HE IS?

PRAY IT:
Jesus, it's so good to pause my life right now and spend some time with You through Your Word. My prayer is that our time together would be pleasing and honoring to You.

READ IT:
Luke 4:14-30

THINK ABOUT IT:
If you had been in the Temple with Jesus that day, how do you think you would have reacted to his claim? Why?

TRY IT:
This will require some courage, but make a plan this week to ask a family member or friend, "Who do you think Jesus really is?"

WRITE IT:
In your own words, complete this prayer in writing: "Jesus, this is who I honestly think you are..."

When Jesus read from the book of Isaiah, he was designating at least two important truths about himself. The first was that he had a specific mission: "to preach good news to the poor..." (verses 17-19), people who are either spiritually or physically poor. Second, by stating that this Scripture had been fulfilled (verse 21), Jesus was claiming he was that promised Messiah. (Remember our earlier readings? If not, revisit readings 24-29.) From biblical times to today, people have had divided opinions on Jesus. Some accept him (verse 22) while others are angered by his claims to be God (verse 28). It sure seems like someone who claimed what Jesus claimed and did what Jesus did is worthy of some type of response. What's yours? Who is Jesus to you?

MEDITATE:

LUKE 4:21-22
He began by saying to them, "Today this scripture is fulfilled in your hearing." All spoke well of him and were amazed at the gracious words that came from his lips. "Isn't this Joseph's son?" they asked.

39 AMAZING AUTHORITY

PRAY IT:
In spite of all that is going on in my life right now, Jesus, I'm eager to read Your Word because I know You have something to say to me. Your Word has the power to change me and I want to be different!

READ IT:
Luke 4:31-44

THINK ABOUT IT:
Imagine what it would have been like to be in the crowd listening to Jesus. How would you have felt? People were amazed by his teaching (32) and amazed by his actions (36)—are you amazed?

TRY IT:
You may not have the healing power of Jesus (40), but you can pray for those who are sick. Pray for those who are hurting and make an effort to let them know that they're in your prayers.

WRITE IT:
List all the things that Jesus did during this section of Scripture. Now, go back and reread verse 42. Write out verse 42 in your own words. Make the connection between what Jesus did with people and how he made sure to spend time alone.

After 30 years of growing up and preparing himself, this passage reveals that Jesus is going public with his ministry. He's starting to travel, teach, heal, and attract crowds (31, 43-44). And as he does, people are amazed (32, 36) with his power and his authority. His authority is seen in both his preaching (32) and in his healing (36). In the midst of all that is going on in Jesus' life there's a quick mention of him spending time alone: "At daybreak Jesus went out to a solitary place" (42). Even Jesus made time to be alone with God in prayer. That relational connection is a source of strength that's still available today.

MEDITATE:

LUKE 4:32
They were amazed at his teaching, because his words had authority.

40 WORTHY OF FOLLOWING

PRAY IT:
Jesus, I ask that You give me a clearer picture of who You really are and who You want to be in my life as I read Your Word today.

READ IT:
Luke 5:1-11

THINK ABOUT IT:
Why do you think Peter would immediately turn the miracle of the fish into a confession of sin? (See verse 8.)

TRY IT:
Ask someone today if they'd be willing to follow Jesus with you. Don't try to "convert" them; simply ask them if they'd be open to learning more about who Jesus is and begin following him by reading about his ways.

WRITE IT:
What do you think about the disciples' response—they "left everything and followed him" (11)? Is that encouraging or discouraging to you? Write out your response.

The fishing nets that were overflowing convinced Peter that he was in the presence of someone unique (8). It's interesting that Peter's first thought wasn't to document the moment and get a picture (or a drawing) of Jesus and Peter arm-in-arm in front of the huge pile of fish. Instead, Peter went straight to the subject of his sin ("I am a sinful man."). That type of response is often the reply of someone having a real spiritual encounter with God. Being in the presence of God's holiness reveals our own sin and corruption. Thankfully, Jesus' message is the same to us as it was to Peter—"Don't be afraid" (10). Jesus came to restore the relationship between sinful humans and a holy God and that's enough reason to leave everything and follow him.

MEDITATE:

LUKE 5:10B-11
Then Jesus said to Simon, "Don't be afraid; from now on you will fish for people." So they pulled their boats up on shore, left everything and followed him.

DISCUSSION QUESTIONS:
THE BEGINNING MINISTRY OF JESUS

PURPOSE:
To review how Jesus was prepared for ministry and to consider temptation and repentance.

QUESTIONS

1. Do you think that God is "pleased" with you (Matthew 3:17)? Why?

2. What claims about Jesus are the most puzzling or offensive to people you know?

3. Jesus was tempted by the devil. Do you think the devil is active today?

4. What can you learn from Jesus in the wilderness about how to resist giving in to temptation? How could you do the same to help with your own temptations?

5. Why do you think the combination of fasting and praying is a healthy spiritual exercise? Have you ever fasted and prayed? What happened?

6. What do you think it means to "follow Jesus" in your life?

7. How would you explain repentance to a friend?

OVERVIEW

THE SERMONS OF JESUS

Most people who hear a sermon on Sunday morning have usually forgotten it by Tuesday—actually, that's being generous; for most of us it's forgotten by Sunday night. You can probably relate to having heard many sermons yourself that you've simply forgotten. They were good; they just didn't stick. Our prayer is that as we dig into some of Jesus' sermons that you'd not forget them, but be motivated to figure out how to live by Jesus' teachings.

In our next five readings we'll read three important sermons of Jesus. The Sermon on the Mount (Matthew 5-7) is the most famous sermon ever preached. Jesus delivered it at the beginning of his public ministry and used it to reveal that his desire for his followers would be radically different than those who lived by the standards of the world. In this sermon, Jesus challenges his followers to be poor in spirit, to be meek, to hunger for righteousness, to be merciful, to be pure in heart, to be committed to peacemaking, and to be willing to endure persecution. That's a lot! He goes on to make radical statements like "love your enemies," "help the needy," "stop worrying about money," and "make God's kingdom your first priority." Yikes! This is a meaty sermon that's very difficult to pull off!

In the second sermon we'll look at, titled "Seven Woes," Jesus lays into some of the religious leaders by getting a little feisty and, in doing so, creates some big-time enemies. He slams these religious folks for not practicing what they preached. But even in the midst of this angry tongue-lashing, Jesus never stops loving his listeners. At the end of one sermon Jesus says, "How often I have longed to gather your children together, as a hen gathers her chicks under her wings, but you were not willing" (Matthew 23:37). Even in his anger, his love is evident.

In the third sermon, Jesus predicts the end of the religious organization of his day and then describes the end of the world. It's pretty wild! Now get ready to listen to the world's greatest preacher... one whose words of truth can change your life.

41 A NEW DAY, A NEW WAY

PRAY IT:
Jesus, I ask that You would open my eyes to the ways that You are at work in the details of my day and life.

READ IT:
Matthew 5:1-48

THINK ABOUT IT:
Which of the Beatitudes (verses 3-10) would you like to have more evident in your life?

TRY IT:
Actually trying to live out Matthew 5:43-44 is radical. Pick out someone you would consider "an enemy" and pray for him/her today. How might you show that person love?

WRITE IT:
There are so many amazing teachings of Jesus in this "Sermon on the Mount." Write out a list of the actions that Jesus is calling us to.

Matthew 5-7 is considered "The Sermon on the Mount" and it's the most famous teaching of Jesus. You could spend your entire life just studying and trying to live out these teachings. In them, Jesus introduces the phrase "Kingdom of Heaven." It's not simply "wait until you die" and you'll go there. First, those who belong to the Kingdom of Heaven have a heart that is committed to the values that are important to God (3-10). Second, note how often Jesus repeats the phrase, "You have heard that it was said before…" (21, 27, 31, 33, 38, 43). Jesus is saying, "It's not good enough to do the right thing [what you were taught before]; [now] you need to do it for the right reason." Those who belong to the Kingdom of Heaven not only have a new heart committed to the values of God, but they also demonstrate that new heart in living differently.

MEDITATE:

MATTHEW 5:14-16
You are the light of the world. A town built on a hill cannot be hidden. Neither do people light a lamp and put it under a bowl. Instead they put it on its stand, and it gives light to everyone in the house. In the same way, let your light shine before others, that they may see your good deeds and glorify your Father in heaven.

42 NOT FOR SHOW

PRAY IT:
Jesus, I don't want to be someone who just knows a lot of information about You and Your Word. I want to be someone who applies it to my life. As I reflect on Your Words please help me also apply them to my life.

READ IT:
Matthew 6:1-34

THINK ABOUT IT:
How often do you perform spiritual actions so others can see rather than performing for an audience of One—Jesus?

TRY IT:
Today, think about what it means for you to seek first his kingdom and his righteousness. Don't simply think about it while you're holding this book open; instead try to make it a thought all day long.

WRITE IT:
Finish writing this sentence: "Jesus, in order to make Your kingdom my first priority, I must..."

This section of Scripture is a continuation of the Sermon on the Mount, and Jesus discusses three vital spiritual actions that he wants us to form as habits—healthy habits. His biggest teaching point seems to be that these habits aren't for "show"... he emphasizes a pure heart. The audience is God, not other humans. The first habit is giving (1-4), the second is prayer (5-15), and the third is fasting (16-18). These habits are not to be done for the eyes of others, but for God and God alone. Jesus concludes with two more topics: money (19-24) and worry (25-34), and ultimately points out that the greatest spiritual habit of all is to seek first his kingdom and his righteousness (33) and that pursuit will put everything else into its proper perspective.

MEDITATE:

MATTHEW 6:33-34
But seek first his kingdom and his righteousness, and all these things will be given to you as well. Therefore do not worry about tomorrow, for tomorrow will worry about itself. Each day has enough trouble of its own.

43 THIS IS NOT EASY!

PRAY IT:
Jesus, I want to follow You and Your ways and I need Your help. Please help me better understand what You would have for me as I continue to read Your Words.

READ IT:
Matthew 7:1-29

THINK ABOUT IT:
When you think deeply about your life, would you say that your life is built more on sand or more on rock? Why?

TRY IT:
Spend a few moments confessing your sins to God. Are there any things that need to be removed from your eyes? (See 7:1-5.)

WRITE IT:
Some of the images that Jesus used to communicate his truths are: sawdust, plank of wood, door, gate, fruit, sand, rock. Which one of these metaphors connected the most with you? Choose one of these words and write a sentence explaining what it meant to you.

There is so much meaty material in the Sermon on the Mount (Matthew 5-7). One could read it over and over and it would always be challenging and convicting—especially within the chapter we just read. Particularly challenging is the whole idea of not judging others! Yikes! Judging others is so easy to do… and sometimes it feels good. There is such a fine line on this issue because, on the one hand, we are called to hate sin while, on the other hand, we are called to love the sinner. This is so much easier said than done. The biggest "ah-ha" of this challenge is to focus on removing our own sins first. If we start by judging our own sin, there won't be much time for pointing out the sins of others.

MEDITATE:

MATTHEW 7:7
Ask and it will be given to you; seek and you will find;
knock and the door will be opened to you.

44 NO MORE MR. NICE GUY

PRAY IT:
Jesus, I deeply want to learn to live in such a way that my life choices match up with my faith. I don't want to pretend to be a Christian or act like someone I'm not. Show me Your way today.

READ IT:
Matthew 23:1-39

THINK ABOUT IT:
Many people accuse the church of being "full of hypocrites." Do you think that's a fair statement? Why or why not?

TRY IT:
Identify the areas within your own life where you are being a hypocrite and then share those areas freely with someone close to you. Ask for prayer and accountability to change those areas of your life.

WRITE IT:
Write down all the names that Jesus calls the religious phonies. Focus on those words and then write down the meaning of "Blind Pharisee" in verse 26: "First clean the inside of the cup and dish, and then the outside also will be clean." What do you think it means to clean the inside of the cup?

In this passage, Jesus is clearly "ticked off." What made him so angry? Simple: hypocrisy. The religious leaders of that time (the teachers of the Law and the Pharisees) weren't living out what they were teaching others to do (3). They thought they were holy, but true holiness doesn't come from a religious title or from "ACTING like a Christian." There are many things people do to appear holy, but that's all it is, an appearance—it's fake, phony, mask-wearing performance. True holiness is when there's consistency between our lifestyle and God's values (23).

MEDITATE:

MATTHEW 23:3
So you must be careful to do everything they tell you. But do not do what they do, for they do not practice what they preach.

45 THE END

PRAY IT:
Jesus, I ask that You would help me see the world and my life from Your perspective as I read Your Word today.

READ IT:
Matthew 24:1-51

THINK ABOUT IT:
What might need to happen in your life to help you focus more on what is "eternal" and less on what is "temporary"? Some things are going to last forever (like your soul) and some things won't last (like your possessions).

TRY IT:
This week, when you hear about wars, political tension, pain, and/or government trouble, pause to be reminded that there will be a day when Jesus comes again, just as he said he would.

WRITE IT:
Write the words "Temporary" and "Eternal" as two headings, then write down areas of your life that might fit under each category. What will not last and what will last?

There are several things in this passage of Scripture that are confusing. You may need to dig into a commentary to understand all that is happening. But, one thing that is clear is that Jesus is predicting the end of the world (15-51). He says it will be a time of great stress and worldwide trouble (which some believe has already begun). But the followers of Jesus will have nothing to fear because they've put their trust in Jesus. Jesus wants us to be ready, watching and waiting for that day (44).

MEDITATE:

MATTHEW 24:36
You also must be ready all the time, for the Son of Man will come when least expected.

DISCUSSION QUESTIONS:
THE SERMONS OF JESUS

PURPOSE:
To review the main themes in the Beatitudes.

QUESTIONS
1. Do you think the Beatitudes (Matthew 5:1-12) are just high standards or do you think we should really try to live that way?

2. Should Christians ever have enemies? Why?

3. Jesus said, "Do not worry about your life..." (Matthew 6:25). What is it that you usually worry about the most?

4. Jesus said, "Do not judge, or you too will be judged" (Matthew 7:1). Is it really possible not to judge others?

5. Can we accept others and still not agree with their behavior? Have you been able to do it?

6. What examples of hypocrisy have you seen in the church? What examples of hypocrisy have you seen in your own life?

7. How should the fact that the world will end and Jesus will return someday affect your life and decisions?

OVERVIEW

THE PARABLES OF JESUS

Everyone loves a good story—young and old alike! Stories tap into our inner child where we are waiting to enjoy and appreciate a good tale that captures our imagination. Our next set of readings are called parables... and parables are a lot like a story. Jesus used these all the time when he was teaching. Parables are a little unique because they don't just come out and display the obvious truth—they often have a hidden meaning that had to be figured out in the midst of the story/parable. Parables kept people interested and engaged, and with Jesus being the master-teacher, he knew how to use good stories and parables to penetrate the heart of his audience.

In our next 5 readings you'll see Jesus doing more story-telling than preaching. Sometimes this story-focused teaching style confused his closest followers to the point where they would ask, "Why do you speak to the people in parables?" (Matthew 13:10).

Jesus understood that stories reached a wide variety of people. Some of Jesus' audience were committed followers, some were his enemies, some were confused onlookers, and some were simply people in pain with hurting souls... but all of them could relate to a good story. Just like you can today!

So whether you're reading these by yourself or talking about them in a group, get ready for some good Jesus stories. You are about to explore the words of the world's greatest teacher as he reveals difficult truths through easy-to-understand stories.

46 WHO IS YOUR NEIGHBOR?

PRAY IT:
Jesus, as I read Your parables may I have eyes to see what You're trying to teach me. I want to uncover the mysteries behind Your words so I can follow them.

READ IT:
Luke 10:25-37

THINK ABOUT IT:
Who was the neighbor in this parable? Who is your neighbor?

TRY IT:
Make it your goal to show mercy in one specific situation this week.

WRITE IT:
After you show mercy (try it), reflect on the situation: Why was it needed? How did you feel? What was the end-result? How might Jesus be changing you through your action?

In this famous parable Jesus attempts to show us the meaning of "neighbor." The Levite and the priest failed to do what the Scriptures taught or what God wants for people who are mistreated. These two "religious" people should have known enough to show mercy and care for the beaten man. They didn't! The twist to Jesus' story is that the person who was the most unlikely to help, the Samaritan (Samaritans were looked down-on during this time), is the one who actually helped. He obeyed the Scriptures and pleased God. Jesus is calling us to go out of our way (at a significant cost) to help those who are helpless.

MEDITATE:

LUKE 10:36-37
"Which of these three do you think was a neighbor to the man who fell into the hands of robbers?" The expert in the law replied, "The one who had mercy on him." Jesus told him, "Go and do likewise."

47 RICH TOWARD GOD

PRAY IT:
Jesus, I am rich in so many ways... maybe not rich with money, but I'm rich in blessings. Help me to better understand the ways that You bless me and help me become rich in You.

READ IT:
Luke 12:13-21

THINK ABOUT IT:
What "things" are important to you? Are they more important to you than the "things of God"?

TRY IT:
Say this prayer every day this week: "God, I thank you for the many material blessings you've given to me. Please show me how I can use them in a way that pleases you."

WRITE IT:
Make a list of some practical ways you can live a life that is "rich toward God" instead of "rich with money."

Jesus illustrates his point with a story about a rich fool (20), which could be summarized like this: "He who dies with the most toys... is still dead." Jesus is making it clear that there's so much more to life than simply gathering money. Our goal in life is not to become rich so we can retire, but our goal as followers of Jesus is to become "rich toward God" (21). That type of richness is one who is generous, willing to share, and loves others (see 1 Timothy 6:18).

MEDITATE:

LUKE 12:21
This is how it will be with whoever stores up things for themselves but is not rich toward God.

48 LET'S PARTY!

PRAY IT:
Jesus, please give me a deeper awareness of Your presence as I read, reflect, and pray.

READ IT:
Luke 14:1-24

THINK ABOUT IT:
In verse 6 we read that "they had nothing to say." When you read of the wisdom of Jesus, are you drawn toward Jesus or are you confused by him?

TRY IT:
Invite someone you wouldn't normally eat with to share a meal with you at school or work. Think of the invitation as caring for him/her in the name of Jesus.

WRITE IT:
What are some common excuses you hear from people who don't want to be part of God's Kingdom? Write down the top three excuses you normally hear.

Jesus teaches about the Kingdom of God with this Parable of the Great Banquet. He makes it clear that God wants all people to get into the banquet and goes to extraordinary trouble to make it possible for everyone to attend (17, 21, 23). Also, we learn that God's kingdom is not just for the wealthy and talented or "together," the banquet host makes a special effort to include those who have troubles too—"the poor, the crippled, the blind and the lame" (21). We also learn that some can and will reject God's invitation to the eternal banquet (18-20, 24).

MEDITATE:

LUKE 14:23-24
Then the master told his servant, "Go out to the roads and country lanes and compel them to come in, so that my house will be full. I tell you, not one of those who were invited will get a taste of my banquet."

49 LOST AND FOUND... AND LOVED

PRAY IT:
Jesus, there have been so many times when I've made a commitment to follow You and then I wind up going my own way—I'm so sorry. Each time You welcome me back. I desperately want to be different and to follow You.

READ IT:
Luke 15:1-32

THINK ABOUT IT:
With which character in the Parable of the Lost Son can you most identify: (1) the younger brother or (2) the older brother? Why?

TRY IT:
Spend some time praying specifically for one of your friends who you know is spiritually lost (separated from God).

WRITE IT:
Write out what feelings are associated with "being lost." What do these parables tell you about the heart of God?

All of us sin (see Romans 3:23), and that sin separates us from a perfect and holy God. Jesus explains this separation with some very visual "lost and found" stories. He told three parables to explain what he meant about being lost as well as revealing the heart of God when they are found. The first two parables, about a lost coin and a lost sheep (verses 3-10), are pretty simple to understand. The third one, about the prodigal son (verses 11-32), is more personal and adds the plot twist of sinful choices. But the theme that runs through all three parables is joy (verses 6-7, 9, 23). God rejoices when sinners repent and turn to him (verses 7, 10).

MEDITATE:

LUKE 15:32
But we had to celebrate and be glad, because this brother of yours was dead and is alive again; he was lost and is found.

50 PRAY... PRAY... PRAY

PRAY IT:
Jesus, You took time to teach Your disciples to pray. I ask that You would help me get a better understanding of how to communicate with You.

READ IT:
Luke 18:1-14

THINK ABOUT IT:
Do you feel that you are really honest with God when you pray?

TRY IT:
Find a place on your phone or computer or notebook where you can begin to write down prayer requests as you think of them throughout the day. Get in the habit of thinking, "I need to talk to Jesus about that!"

WRITE IT:
Write out your prayer when you're ready to end your time with today's reading.

Jesus uses these two parables to teach about prayer. In the Persistent Widow Parable (1-8), Jesus uses the woman as a model for effective prayer because she's begging, pleading, and doesn't stop. Notice that she's not praying for money or a car or more possessions; she's praying for justice (3)—which is consistent with God's heart. In the parable about the Pharisee and the tax collector (9-14), the obvious point is that God responds to the prayers of humility rather than arrogance. Being involved in church, avoiding sin, and pursuing spiritual disciples are all good things... unless they cause you to become arrogant and look down on others. God responds to the humble.

MEDITATE:

LUKE 18:14B
For all those who exalt themselves will be humbled, and those who humble themselves will be exalted.

DISCUSSION QUESTIONS:
THE PARABLES OF JESUS

PURPOSE:
To review and understand what we learn from Jesus' parables.

QUESTIONS

1. Are there times when showing mercy might not be the right thing to do? When? Have you experienced any? What examples of showing mercy have you seen or experienced?

2. What are practical ways that you can be generous toward God?

3. How could you use the resources God has given you for maximum return according to his priorities?

4. What practical steps could you take to show more compassion?

5. Was there ever a time in your life when you felt lost and far from God? What was it like? Have you made your way back to him yet? If so, how did it happen?

6. Can pride ever be a good thing? How do you know when pride is bad? How can you avoid it?

7. What do you think makes prayer "work"?

OVERVIEW

MORE PARABLES OF JESUS

In our next five readings, we'll cover another set of parables based on two topics. The first is maybe the greatest theme that arises from Jesus' parables: "the Kingdom of Heaven." We've already established a basic definition of that mysterious phrase. It means "God's rule on the earth" (see reading 41), but that sounds too much like a quote from a churchy book. Thankfully, we'll better understand Jesus' meaning of the "Kingdom of Heaven" when we read the stories Jesus told.

As you read, notice that Jesus never said, "The Kingdom of Heaven is exactly this... period!" Instead, he said, "The Kingdom of Heaven is like..." and then he connected it to a good, short story. That's because there is so much to understand about the Kingdom of Heaven. Each of the ten parables about the Kingdom of Heaven (I know, ten is a lot, but some are very short so we'll read several at a time) gives us a different insight into this major theme. Then, at the end, you'll need to piece everything together. It will be like assembling a jigsaw puzzle; after a little while you will begin to see the full picture more clearly.

The second topic in this section of readings is actually a slightly different teaching method than the traditional parable. Jesus called it a "figure of speech" (see John 10:6). Instead of telling a full story with a plot and a punch line, he pointed his listeners to familiar objects like a gate, a vine, some branches, a gardener, a shepherd, and a flock of sheep—and he used those "figures" to explain a deeper truth.

So, whether it's a story or figure of speech, there's a lot to learn from the parables of Jesus. So, read slowly... Take it all in... Write down your questions and enjoy learning more from God's Word. And, if you're doing this as part of a group, enjoy being with others while you're at it... What a cool thing.

51 IT'S LIKE...

PRAY IT:
God, please do whatever is necessary in me so that I can receive Your Word into my life and allow it to grow and flourish.

READ IT:
Matthew 13:1-58

THINK ABOUT IT:
Which of the four soils (verses 4-8) best represents your heart?

TRY IT:
Go outside and pick up a handful of soil where plants are growing well. Remind yourself that you want to be "good soil" where God's Word can take root and grow.

WRITE IT:
As a follower of Jesus, there's a good chance that you'll return to the Parable of the Four Soils several times to explain how God's Word is often received. To help with your memory, write down each of the four soils and come up with a one-word definition for each one.

Jesus packs a lot of information about the Kingdom of Heaven in these six short parables. As you reflect on them, be reminded of the basic definition of the Kingdom of Heaven (see Reading 41): Those who belong to the Kingdom of Heaven not only have a new heart committed to the values of God, but they also demonstrate that new heart by living differently. When all these parables are put together, they help create a clearer picture of the Kingdom of Heaven. It starts small (like seeds), has power to grow (like a mustard seed or yeast), is valuable and worthy of pursuit (like hidden treasure or a pearl), and will eventually include many people (like a net). The only bummer to this picture is that some will oppose the Kingdom of Heaven and its people (like weeds).

MEDITATE:

MATTHEW 13:10-13
The disciples came to him and asked, "Why do you speak to the people in parables?" He replied, "Because the knowledge of the secrets of the kingdom of heaven has been given to you, but not to them. Whoever has will be given more, and they will have an abundance. Whoever does not have, even what they have will be taken from them. This is why I speak to them in parables."

52 HOW GENEROUS!

PRAY IT:
I open my heart to You, Jesus… Speak into it today through Your Word and continue the inner transformation that You have planned for my heart.

READ IT:
Matthew 20:1-16

THINK ABOUT IT:
If you were one of the first workers, would you be angry or "okay" with others making as much as you made and only working one hour?

TRY IT:
Like the landowner in the parable, you have the right to be generous with your money. Consider one way you could bless someone with your generosity this week… and then do it.

WRITE IT:
Write your response to this statement: "Salvation can't be earned by my efforts: it's a free gift from God."

The parable seems easy to understand: workers are hired at different points throughout the day with the promise of fair wages at the end of their work shift. But those who worked 12 hours are paid the same as those who worked 1 hour. Most likely, Jesus tells a story that seems "unfair" to get his audience thinking about God's generosity. The gift of salvation and being part of the Kingdom of Heaven cannot be earned—no matter how hard you work. Salvation is a free gift from God (see Ephesians 2:8-9). Jesus is trying to help us understand that salvation is based on God's generosity, not on how long or hard or good our work is. God is generous because he wants everyone to enjoy the benefits of his Kingdom.

MEDITATE:

MATTHEW 20:16
So the last will be first, and the first will be last.

53 THE RETURN OF JESUS... GET READY

PRAY IT:
Jesus, I want to be ready for what You have for me, both today and in the future. As I stop to dig into Your Word, would You please reveal Your desire for me today?

READ IT:
Matthew 25:1-46

THINK ABOUT IT:
How do you feel about there being a final day of judgment when Jesus will someday return to judge humanity?

TRY IT:
While these parables reveal Jesus' second coming, the Sheep and Goats Parable reveals that our faith must be lived out through acts of compassion (35-45). The Apostle James referred to this same idea many years later (see James 2:26). Make it a goal to intentionally show compassion to someone today.

WRITE IT:
These parables refer to Jesus' second coming. Write down what you think it might look like to be "ready."

Earlier, Jesus made the point that God invites everyone into his kingdom. Now he says some won't accept that invitation; some will be left out and it won't be God's fault. The ten virgins all had an opportunity to get ready for the bridegroom; five used it wisely and five squandered it (1-13). All three of the servants received an investment from the wealthy man; two made the most of it and one didn't (14-30). The last parable reveals a Day of Judgment when Jesus will determine who will enter the Kingdom of Heaven and who will not.

MEDITATE:

MATTHEW 25:37-40
Then the righteous will answer him, "Lord, when did we see you hungry and feed you, or thirsty and give you something to drink? When did we see you a stranger and invite you in, or needing clothes and clothe you? When did we see you sick or in prison and go to visit you?" The King will reply, "Truly I tell you, whatever you did for one of the least of these brothers and sisters of mine, you did for me."

54 THE GOOD SHEPHERD

PRAY IT:
Jesus, I desperately want to hear Your voice. Please help me listen with my heart as I spend time with You and Your Word.

READ IT:
John 10:1-18

THINK ABOUT IT:
Do you think Jesus is saying that he is the only way for people to get to God?

TRY IT:
If you aren't familiar with the job responsibilities of a shepherd, spend a few minutes to research (Google) them to deepen your understanding of the meaning of this parable.

WRITE IT:
List the job description of a shepherd. What might be some connections between the shepherd and God?

In today's reading, we see Jesus using two figures of speech to teach about himself: (1) a gate to a sheep pen, and (2) a good shepherd. The gate analogy is very direct: Jesus is the entry point into God's Kingdom (9). Then, he calls himself "The Good Shepherd" and he emphasizes two important details—the first is the shepherd's voice. Jesus' followers can enjoy a close relationship with him (14) and they will recognize his voice (4-5). As a follower of Jesus, he knows your name (3) and cares for you like a shepherd cares for his sheep. And, the second detail is that the shepherd is willing to sacrifice himself for the sheep (11, 15). Jesus is clearly painting a picture of what he would later do on the cross as his ultimate sacrificial act.

MEDITATE:

JOHN 10:10
The thief comes only to steal and kill and destroy; I have come that they might have life, and have it to the full.

55 I'M A BRANCH!

PRAY IT:
Jesus, I am so thankful that You are in charge of both this world as well as in charge of my life. I come into Your presence today confident that You know what's best for me. I give You my heart to be molded by You.

READ IT:
John 15:1-17

THINK ABOUT IT:
"Bearing fruit" seems like an odd phrase. What do you think it looks like to bear fruit?

TRY IT:
When you walk by a plant or bush today, grab a dead leaf or branch and put it in your pocket or backpack. Then put it in a place around your house where it will remind you of Jesus' words about staying connected to him for a life of fruitfulness.

WRITE IT:
Draw something that will remind you of the principle of the branch and the vine. Remember to include the Gardener.

The context of today's reading is near the end of Jesus' earthly life. He is communicating some of the most important truths that he wants his followers to get—the relationship with his Father and with his followers. To do this, Jesus used a familiar image—a vine and branches. Jesus is the vine (1), his followers are the branches (5), and God is the gardener (1). Then, Jesus goes on to emphasize two other specific points: (1) the primary job of a branch (his followers) is to bear fruit (do the things he's instructed them to do) (7-8) and (2) love. He commanded followers to love one another (17). Without being connected to the vine (remaining connected to him), bearing true fruit and expressing genuine love is impossible (4).

MEDITATE:

JOHN 15:5
I am the vine; you are the branches. If you remain in me and I in you, you will bear much fruit; apart from me you can do nothing.

DISCUSSION QUESTIONS:
MORE PARABLES OF JESUS

PURPOSE:
To review and understand what we learn from more of Jesus' parables.

QUESTIONS

1. In your own words, how would you define the "Kingdom of Heaven"?

2. Why do you think most of the religions of the world are based on the idea that we can somehow earn salvation?

3. If salvation is really a gift from God, does it matter what we do? Why bother to do right things and display character and be good if you can't earn salvation?

4. Some people are offended by the idea that Jesus is the only way to God. What do you think?

5. What would you say to a person who insists that there are many ways to God?

6. What does it mean for a Christian to "bear fruit"? Should all believers bear the same kind of fruit? Is there some fruit that all followers of Christ should have?

7. How do most people define love? How would you explain real love? Are the two definitions different?

OVERVIEW

THE MIRACLES OF JESUS

In our next batch of readings, we'll look specifically at the miracles of Jesus. The first set of miracles could be called "supernatural events." These miracles were things like: (1) changing water into wine, (2) calming the seas, (3) feeding the 5,000, (4) walking on water, and (5) causing a fig tree to wither. All big-time stuff! Actually, all of Jesus' miracles could be called supernatural, but these five reveal Jesus' power over the forces of nature.

In the second set of miracles, we'll cover six healing miracles of Jesus. Once we've completed these readings we'll see why the miracles are such an important part of Jesus' ministry and to the validation of the fact that he was who he said he was—God-in-the-flesh.

Jesus seemed to perform these miracles for a variety of reasons. He wanted to meet the needs of those around him: his disciples, the crowds, and the individual followers he encountered along the way. But beyond that, Jesus' miracles were "signs" that would reveal that Jesus was actually God. This reality would help people put their faith in him as God. Miracles are not just interesting to read, they're important for an increased faith.

So whether you're reading on your own or discussing this in a group with others, may your faith be more enhanced as you become more aware of God's power.

56 NEW WINE

PRAY IT:
Jesus, I not only want to read and better understand Your miracles, I want to experience the miracle of my life being changed to be more like Yours. I can't do that on my own. I need the miracle of a new birth.

READ IT:
John 2:1-11

THINK ABOUT IT:
Why do you think Jesus didn't want to show off his power?

TRY IT:
Today, when you drink something, pause to thank God that he not only has the power to turn water into wine but he has the power to change your life. Make sure to thank him.

WRITE IT:
List three areas from your life that you would like for Jesus to change from old (water) into new (wine).

It seems as though Mary and Jesus had two different plans that were important to them. Mary wanted her son to "save the day" and Jesus had a bigger plan in play when he said, "My time has not yet come" (4). Jesus had come to fulfill the mission given to him by his heavenly Father, not his earthly mother. But, what's the significance of Jesus' first miracle? John adds a comment at the end of the passage to make sure his readers get the point (11): Jesus performed miracles because they "revealed his glory," that is, they were evidence of his divine nature (Jesus was God). But second, they helped people, in this case his disciples, "put their faith in him." Jesus' mission was to help people believe that he was the Son of God.

MEDITATE:

JOHN 2:11
What Jesus did here in Cana of Galilee was the first of the signs through which he revealed his glory; and his disciples believed in him.

57 NO FEAR!

PRAY IT:
Jesus, I know You have power over everything and yet I so often lack faith in You. When I go through storms in my life, I pray that You would remind me of Your power. I want to learn to rely on You and not worry so much.

READ IT:
Mark 4:35-41

THINK ABOUT IT:
What are your biggest fears? Or, what do you worry about the most?

TRY IT:
Spend a little additional time talking to God about some of the things you fear. Ask him to help you replace those fears with a stronger faith in his control of your life.

WRITE IT:
Make a list of five things that you worry about. Revisit that list every day this week and ask God to help you grow in your faith.

The fear within that boat must have been incredible. It took a lot for seasoned fisherman to be scared. Fear is a common part of life. At some point, fear is natural for everyone. Most of our fear comes from constant worry. What's difficult for followers of Jesus to learn is that once we belong to Jesus, it doesn't matter what happens in life, and it doesn't matter how bad things get. Jesus has the power to change not only the wind and the waves, but also every force at work in our lives. Fear is real, but so is faith. When your faith becomes stronger, fear will become weaker.

MEDITATE:

MARK 4:41
They were terrified and asked each other, "Who is this? Even the wind and the waves obey him!"

58 MIRACLE MEAL

PRAY IT:
Jesus, I look forward to good meals and filling my stomach—that comes so naturally to me. I want to learn to eagerly look forward to times with You knowing that You fill my very real and deep needs.

READ IT:
Matthew 14:13-21

THINK ABOUT IT:
How do you think the disciples felt before, during, and after this miracle?

TRY IT:
When you eat your next meal today, pause and reflect on how well you are fed. Thank God not only for your food, but also for feeding you spiritually.

WRITE IT:
What is something that is so big in your life that you know you desperately need God's help? Write it down. Next to the words you just wrote, write: "Seek the Kingdom of God above all else, and live righteously, and he will give you everything you need." (Matthew 6:33, NLT).

As exciting as it may have been to be a disciple of Jesus, it must also have been very difficult too. Jesus was constantly testing, teaching, questioning, and pushing these guys into tough situations. He appears to deeply care that they understand faith and God's power. That's what is going on in this familiar miracle. Jesus already knows he can feed the 5,000+ people (verse 21). But before he does, he challenges the disciples to solve the problem on their own (verse 16). What about you? What's your first instinct when you face a big problem? Do you make a plan? Do you complain? Do you become fearful? In the midst of this food-less situation, Jesus says, "Bring them here to me" (verse 18). In other words, "Remember who I am and look to me first."

MEDITATE:

MATTHEW 14:14
When Jesus landed and saw a large crowd, he had compassion on them and healed their sick.

59 TAKING THE FIRST STEP

PRAY IT:
Jesus, I'm often filled with fear and I ask that You help me become a person who trusts in You rather than trusting in my own power. I want the peace that comes from trusting in You.

READ IT:
Matthew 14:22-33

THINK ABOUT IT:
Would you have gotten out of the boat? Why or why not?

TRY IT:
Today, do something you normally would be too afraid to do. Before you do, focus on Jesus, have a conversation with him, admit your fear, and then feel what it's like to step out on faith.

WRITE IT:
Write these words someplace where you'll see them every day: "Take courage! It is I. Don't be afraid." —Jesus

Some miracles are hard to believe and explain. To doubters, you could say, "I don't fully understand everything, but I know Jesus has saved me, and I've experienced his ability to take away my fear. So, to me, it doesn't seem so unbelievable that he could also walk on water. I've experienced enough of Jesus to know that I don't need to see it to believe it." Just because you haven't seen something happen doesn't mean it couldn't be true. Peter had never seen a man walking on water either; it might have been a mirage or a ghost or something worse. Still, he stepped out of the boat. That's faith! It's the willingness to move forward, trusting Jesus even when the way is unclear or frightening. Peter's step of faith led to failure... at first. But the strong grip of Jesus clarified that it was no ghost—it was Jesus.

MEDITATE:

MATTHEW 14:27
But Jesus immediately said to them:
"Take courage! It is I. Don't be afraid."

60 SERIOUS FRUIT

PRAY IT:
Jesus, I pray that You will give me new life today as I read Your Word and think about Your ways.

READ IT:
Matthew 21:18-22

THINK ABOUT IT:
Do you really believe prayer is powerful? Or, is it simply important?

TRY IT:
Set a prayer goal (how often and when) and commit yourself to learn to pray "bigger prayers" and to pray "normal prayers" throughout the day. You can talk to God everywhere, all the time.

WRITE IT:
Start a list in your prayer journal that you title "Mountain Prayers." These are the biggies! These are the ones that seem impossible and feel like they will require a miracle. Begin to pray for these biggies.

This seems like such a weird miracle! Jesus getting mad at a tree—seems a little uncharacteristic of Jesus. It appears as though Jesus wanted his closest followers to understand that bearing fruit is serious business and there's no time to waste. As we've discovered in our reading journey, bearing fruit is a big deal to Jesus. Our job is to stay connected to the vine (see Reading 55). A connection to the vine produces fruit. Staying connected to Jesus appears to involve at least two things: faith and prayer. This means faith built on a deep and trusting relationship with Jesus and prayer built on trust that God will accomplish his purposes in our lives.

MEDITATE:

MATTHEW 21:22
If you believe, you will receive whatever you ask for in prayer.

DISCUSSION QUESTIONS:
THE MIRACLES OF JESUS

PURPOSE:
To understand what miracles are and discuss how Jesus' miracles impact our lives.

QUESTIONS

1. How would you define a miracle? Do you think they still happen? Have you ever experienced one?

2. What are the biggest fears that people face? How could Jesus help?

3. Can you think of a time in your life when you were overwhelmed by fear? What happened and what helped you get through it? How has faith in Jesus helped you?

4. Some people say that if you have enough faith, anything is possible. Do you agree? Why?

5. When have you taken a big step of faith? What happened and what did you learn?

6. How would you make "the case for Christ"? For you, what are the strongest proofs that Jesus was the Son of God?

7. How important is it that Jesus performed the miracles in these passages? Would you believe in him just as strongly if he had not?

OVERVIEW

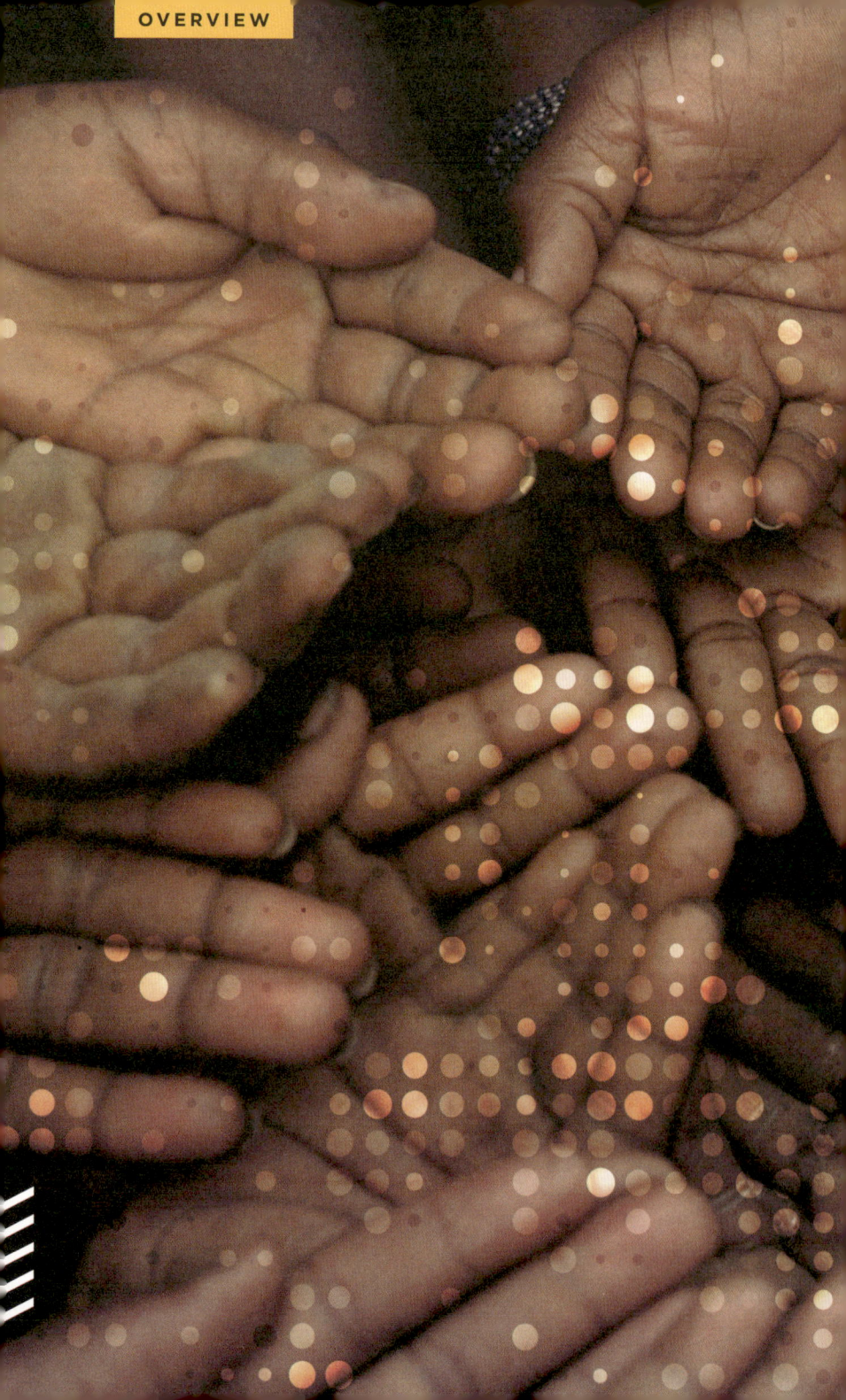

MORE MIRACLES OF JESUS

It's no secret that not everyone believes in the miracle of healing—some do and some don't. The challenge for us in the next five readings is to examine the healing miracles of Jesus with an open mind. We'll read how Jesus: (1) caused a blind man to see, (2) made a paralyzed man able to walk, (3) restored a demon-possessed man back to normal, (4) cured a woman with a hopeless bleeding problem, and (5) brought two dead people back to life. That's right—dead, back to life.

These healing miracles are awesome and definitely some of the most exciting and inspiring moments of Jesus' earthly ministry. These healing miracles also give us a deeper understanding of the heart of Jesus. He had compassion for people and wasn't too busy or important to help people overcome their problems. These miracles also reveal his power, not just over sickness, but also over sin. Most importantly, these healings provide more evidence that Jesus was who he said he was... the Son of God.

There's a lot to these miracles, so let's read through them one-by-one, and as you do, imagine that you're there. Think about yourself as a follower of Jesus who has a front-row seat to these amazing events. Think about what you would have said or felt or done had you been there. Put yourself into the story so you can experience the healing ministry of Jesus. If you're reading this as part of a group, share your feelings with one another. Whether you're reading this alone or discussing it as a group, Jesus is waiting to do a miracle in your life.

61 I SAW THE LIGHT

PRAY IT:
Jesus, there are many times I walk through my day being blind to how You are at work. I close my eyes to Your goodness and miss the ways You're working around me. I beg You to help me see what You see in others.

READ IT:
John 9:1-41

THINK ABOUT IT:
Some people simply reject the truth about Jesus. They did it during Jesus' time and they do it today. Why do you think Jesus is so controversial?

TRY IT:
Walk around your house with your eyes closed for a few minutes. When you open your eyes stop for a minute and thank God for some of the things that you take for granted (like sight).

WRITE IT:
Finish this statement, "Once I was blind (spiritually), but now I see. Before I was 'healed' by Jesus, I used to…"

Why is it so difficult for some to accept the fact that Jesus heals people? When told about Jesus healing the bind man, the Pharisees [religious leaders] dismissed it on a technicality—working on the Sabbath (16). The blind man was the only one who saw the true Light of the World (5). Instead of questioning or challenging Jesus, the healed man simply obeyed and followed Jesus' instructions (7). Next, he honestly shared his experience with others (11, 25), even defending his encounter with Jesus in spite of the pressure they used against him (24-34). Finally, after taking time to think it through, he put his faith in Jesus (38).

MEDITATE:

JOHN 9:25
He replied, "Whether he is a sinner or not, I don't know. One thing I do know. I was blind but now I see!"

62 THE POWER OF FRIENDSHIP

PRAY IT:
Jesus, there are areas of my life that need healing, some I know of and other areas that are either hidden or I'm ignoring. I need Your healing today. I want to be used by You to help bring healing to others near me.

READ IT:
Luke 5:17-26

THINK ABOUT IT:
Do you have the types of friends who would sacrifice to help you get healed?

TRY IT:
Invite a friend to church or youth group or a Christian club on campus. Make it a goal to bring that friend to hear more about Jesus.

WRITE IT:
List two ways that you could take a step of faith on behalf of someone close to you.

What a scene this must have created around town and within that house! It must have been very difficult to carry a paralyzed man across town. It took four men to lift him. These friends did this for at least two reasons. First, they loved their friend and expressed it by their sacrificial effort. And second, they believed Jesus could make a difference in their friend's life. It also took faith, as Jesus pointed out (verse 20). It's interesting to note that Jesus healed the man because of "their faith." It wasn't just the paralyzed man's faith, it was their faith—a community of friends. Sometimes God answers prayers based on the collective faith of others—that's a powerful thought for a group of friends.

MEDITATE:

LUKE 5:26
Everyone was amazed and gave praise to God. They were filled with awe and said, "We have seen remarkable things today."

63 GOD'S ENEMY

PRAY IT:
Jesus, I know there are evil forces at work in the world and I'm thankful that You're powerful enough to defeat them.

READ IT:
Mark 5:1-20

THINK ABOUT IT:
Do you think demon possession is real in today's world? Why or why not?

TRY IT:
Share with someone this week what you wrote in the "Write It" section.

WRITE IT:
Jesus told the healed man to "tell them how much the Lord has done for you." Write out a summary of what Jesus has done for you.

Throughout the Bible we learn that God's enemy (the devil) is real. In today's reading, it's sad to know that the devil had been at work in this poor guy's life for a long time. He tortured his mind and body and separated the man from his true self as well as his community of friends. But Jesus wasn't about to let that continue to happen. First, Jesus took control of the situation and of the demons (6-8). Next, Jesus dealt with the demons once and for all (11-13), something the townspeople had never been able to do (4). And finally, Jesus restored the man and gave him a renewed purpose in life (18-20). It's a great display of the power of God—the healed man wants to follow Jesus.

MEDITATE:

MARK 5:19
Jesus... said, "Go home to your own people and tell them how much the Lord has done for you, and how he has had mercy on you."

64 DOING WHAT IT TAKES

PRAY IT:
Jesus, please help me to understand all that I can from Your Word and to learn to better trust and believe what I can't understand. I know You can heal areas of my life that are incomplete. I need You today... and every day!

READ IT:
Mark 5:21-43

THINK ABOUT IT:
Jesus encourages the faith of the woman and challenges Jairus to "just believe." Do you think faith is always a necessary part of being healed?

TRY IT:
Bring the area of your life where you feel the greatest sense of hopelessness to God in prayer. Consider positioning yourself on your knees with an attitude of humility and desperation.

WRITE IT:
Write out some of the feelings that you think Jairus might have had while he was waiting for Jesus to heal the woman. After that, circle the words that best fit you when you're waiting for Jesus to meet your needs.

Our reading today weaves together the accounts of two miracles that occurred during an exciting and chaotic time in Jesus' ministry. The Gospels reveal that everywhere Jesus went he drew a crowd. People were amazed at him and his teachings. First, an unnamed woman, who had suffered from uncontrollable bleeding for twelve years (25), slipped through the crowd simply to touch Jesus. Her friends may have criticized her desperate attempt at healing (28), but Jesus met her boldness with, "Your faith has healed you" (34). Sometimes faith requires us to take desperate actions. Next, the daughter of Jairus, a man who would have normally been against Jesus, was sick. Jairus would have been criticized by his friends as a traitor to turn to Jesus for help. Once again Jesus meets his needs and says, "Don't be afraid; just believe" (verse 36). Sometimes faith requires us to ignore what others think.

MEDITATE:

MARK 5:34
He said to her, "Daughter, your faith has healed you. Go in peace and be freed from your suffering."

65 RESURRECTION POWER

PRAY IT:

Jesus, bring me life today as I read Your Word, reflect on Your ways, and consider my actions. I want my life to reflect being a follower of You.

READ IT:

John 11:1-45

THINK ABOUT IT:

The Bible teaches that the resurrection of Jesus was the ultimate proof that Jesus was who he said he was—God (see 1 Corinthians 15:1-34). Why do you think your faith was built on the resurrection?

TRY IT:

This week, use Martha's words as your prayer: "Yes, Lord, I believe that you are the Christ, the Son of God, who has come into the world."

WRITE IT:

List three ways that Jesus revealed the power of God through the event that you just read in John 11.

Jesus made a very bold statement that he was the resurrection and the life (25-26). That was a radical claim and many wanted to kill him because of those words. But, as followers of Jesus, we now understand what an incredible promise it is to us. The resurrection is the foundation of our faith! It's the proof that Jesus defeated death (see 1 Corinthians 15:1-34). Believing in Jesus, his death on the cross, and his resurrection is the belief that brings eternal life (see John 14:6). This miraculous raising of Lazarus as well as the raising of Jairus's daughter (Reading 64) were early signs of the greatest resurrection that was soon to come.

MEDITATE:

JOHN 11:25-26

Jesus said to her, "I am the resurrection and the life. The one who believes in me will live, even though they die; and whoever lives by believing in me will never die. Do you believe this?"

DISCUSSION QUESTIONS:
MORE MIRACLES OF JESUS

PURPOSE:
To discuss more of Jesus' miracles and their impact on our lives.

QUESTIONS

1. Why do you think people are skeptical about miracles today? Do you think faith and science are compatible? Explain.

2. Do you think it's possible to be possessed by demons? How do you feel about movies or television programs about demon possession? Why?

3. What keeps more people from trusting Jesus, especially with their hurts and needs?

4. How could you encourage your friends to trust Jesus? Do you think it's your responsibility?

5. Why is it important that Jesus raised Jairus's daughter and Lazarus from the dead? What did that signal to the religious leaders of that time? What does it signal to you?

6. How does knowing that Jesus has power over death help you think about death and dying?

7. What do these miracles tell you about Jesus?

OVERVIEW

THE PRAYERS OF JESUS

Prayer is something everyone has tried and yet no one fully understands. The most repeated prayer of all time is probably, "God, help me!" But probably the most powerful prayer is the one Jesus taught that begins, "Our Father, Who art in heaven, hallowed be Thy name..." These words come from what is known as the "Lord's Prayer," and it's a pretty short prayer, but it's a very specific and powerful example of talking to God. In these next five readings we will look closely at the greatest "pray-er" (Jesus) the world has ever known.

After observing Jesus pray, one of the disciples boldly said, "Lord, teach us to pray..." (Luke 11:1). What a great statement! If you want to learn how to pray, watch someone who knows how to do it. Thankfully, for us there's no better teacher than Jesus.

Jesus prayed in all kinds of situations—he prayed spontaneous prayers when good things happened in his ministry (see Luke 10:1-24). He prayed long, formal prayers when he had big issues on his mind (see John 17:1-26). And Jesus prayed short, intense prayers when he was under great pressure (see Mark 14:32-42).

But, why did Jesus pray? As the Son of God, he had all God's power and could do anything he wanted. But Jesus' prayers were more like conversations with God the Father. That relationship was the most important one to him and that's why he spent so much time talking, listening, and simply spending time in God's presence conversing with him.

Perhaps the greatest lesson we can learn is that Jesus didn't pray just at set times or special occasions; he prayed whenever he could (see Mark 1:29-39). Jesus was constantly praying, and as you're about to read, prayer was essential for Jesus. And if that's true, imagine how much more essential prayer is for you and me today.

For those of you reading in groups, make sure you spend some time praying... praying like Jesus.

66 ESCAPING TO PRAY

PRAY IT:
Jesus, in spite of all the stuff going on in my life that seems so important, my heart's desire is to deepen my relationship with You. I want to know You in deeper ways.

READ IT:
Mark 1:29-39

THINK ABOUT IT:
Why do you think Jesus wanted to be by himself? Do you think he felt the pressure of others? ("Everyone is looking for you!" See verse 37.)

TRY IT:
Experiment with a different approach to prayer today. For example, even if you are alone, pray aloud, or try a different posture (kneeling), or go outside and look at the sky as you pray, or take "a prayer walk," or...

WRITE IT:
Write your response to this statement: "For most, prayer is something we make time for in the middle of our busy lives. For Jesus, prayer was central to his life. He didn't make time for prayer, he made time for everything else."

It would be a great goal to learn to pray more like Jesus. He obviously is the Master at how to live life and he was in constant communication with God the Father. In today's reading, we get a snapshot into some of his prayer habits/actions. There could be some learnings for us: He prayed early. Jesus got up "while it was still dark" to pray. This doesn't mean we should only pray in the morning, but prayer was the first thing on Jesus' mind. He prayed without distraction. Even Jesus needed to get to a "solitary place" to avoid people/noise/distraction. He prayed no matter what. Everyone was looking for Jesus (37) and people had unmet needs and Jesus was in high-demand, yet he "escaped" in spite of the disciples' pressure. There's always pressure to get busy with the day... but, we can learn to make prayer part of our entire day.

MEDITATE:

MARK 1:38
Jesus replied, "Let us go somewhere else—to the nearby villages—so I can preach there also. That is why I have come."

67 JOYFUL PRAYER

PRAY IT:
Today my prayer is that I would, in some small way, experience the joy that Your disciples experience when they were with You, Jesus. May I have eyes to see and ears to hear what You want me to see and hear.

READ IT:
Luke 10:1-24

THINK ABOUT IT:
What do you think is the point of prayer?

TRY IT:
Try to pray and make your entire prayer a prayer of praise. Don't allow it to turn to you or your needs. Instead just pray by giving God praise.

WRITE IT:
Make a list of some of the things that bring you joy.

The 72 "missionaries" had returned with great results and stories (17) and you can almost imagine Jesus giving "high fives" as he hears their reports. Then, in the middle of this time, Jesus begins to pray (21). Notice the emphasis on joy. There was reason for joy because the work of the missionaries was bearing fruit, but there was also reason for joy because Satan was being defeated (18) and God's way was becoming more clear to the most unlikely people (21). Too often, we reduce prayer to our list of problems and worries and don't include praise with a joyful heart. God definitely cares about our list, but Jesus clearly illustrates that there's more to prayer than requests. Prayer also includes joy, praise, and celebration for who God is and what he's doing.

MEDITATE:

LUKE 10:21
At that time Jesus, full of joy through the Holy Spirit, said, "I praise you, Father, Lord of heaven and earth, because you have hidden these things from the wise and learned, and revealed them to little children. Yes, Father, for this is what you were pleased to do."

68 THE SCHOOL OF PRAYER

PRAY IT:
I want to learn to pray in a way that is so natural and life-giving. Right now, I feel like I'm such a beginner with prayer and have so much to learn. Teach me, Jesus, to draw closer to You in my communication.

READ IT:
Luke 11:1-13

THINK ABOUT IT:
Do you think the answering of prayer is as simple as Jesus makes it sound in verse 9 ("Ask and it will be given to you...")?

TRY IT:
Close your eyes and imagine that Jesus is actually sitting with you in the room. What chair is he sitting in? How do you feel? What are you thinking? Now, talk to him.

WRITE IT:
Paraphrase the Lord's Prayer—write it in your own language—in a way that makes most sense to you.

If someone asked you to help him/her develop a deeper prayer life (1), how would you respond? By explaining your prayer habits, by sharing a book on prayer, or perhaps by suggesting a helpful seminar? Jesus begins his response by simply praying. The Lord's Prayer is the most famous and most repeated prayer in history. It's so short and yet so deep. A couple thoughts to consider: first, in prayer we must look beyond ourselves to God, his character, his holiness, his kingdom, and his will (2). Second, we can pray about our day-to-day needs—food, forgiveness, and strength to avoid temptation (3-4). After the example of prayer, Jesus also encourages us to be bold and persistent when we pray (5-10). Jesus teaches that faith in God, combined with a bold persistence in prayer, will lead to incredible results (Matthew 17:20-21).

MEDITATE:

LUKE 11:9-10
So I say to you: Ask and it will be given to you; seek and you will find; knock and the door will be opened to you. For everyone who asks receives; the one who seeks finds; and to the one who knocks, the door will be opened.

69 A DEFINING PRAYER

PRAY IT:
Jesus, I thank You for loving me deeply. I'm grateful that You don't take Your love away from me. I want to be more consistent in my prayers and conversation with You. Help me know You better.

READ IT:
John 17:1-26

THINK ABOUT IT:
In John 17:13, Jesus uses the words "my joy"... He is not talking about a happy feeling. So, what do you think he's talking about?

TRY IT:
If you knew you were leaving earth tomorrow, how would you pray? Think deeply about that specific prayer.

WRITE IT:
Write out your "Try It" prayer.

Jesus had just given his anxious disciples their final instructions (see John 13-16). Now, he moves into this long prayer where he prays for himself, for the disciples, and for everyone. Jesus begins by praying for himself (1-5) because "the time has come" (1) for him to complete his mission on earth as a human. Jesus then prays for his disciples (6-19) and asks for three things. First, they'll need God's protection (11, 15). Second, he prays that the disciples would have "my joy" (13). Finally, he prays that they be set apart and transformed to be like Jesus. Jesus finishes by praying for the unity of all who would believe in him as a result of the disciples' message (20-26).

MEDITATE:

JOHN 17:3
Now this is eternal life: that they know you, the only true God, and Jesus Christ, whom you have sent.

70 PRESSURE PRAYER

PRAY IT:
Jesus, I am hungry to grow. Please feed me on Your Word today. You have the words of life that can nourish my soul and help my faith grow.

READ IT:
Mark 14:32-42

THINK ABOUT IT:
Can you think of a time when you were under a lot of pressure? Did the pressure change the intensity of your prayers?

TRY IT:
It's not unusual to be stressed out and begin to worry instead of pray. Ask your closest friend to ask about your prayer times when you're most pressured. Best friends have a way of knowing when we're acting different, pressured, or stressed.

WRITE IT:
Complete this sentence: I feel most pressure when...

This may be the most intense prayer that Jesus prayed (at least one that we're made aware of). How did Jesus pray when he was under pressure? The answer is packed into a single verse (36). He starts by calling out to his Father. The word *Abba* literally means "daddy." Next, he makes a statement he knows to be true: "All things are possible for God." Jesus then makes his request: "Take this cup from me"; in other words, "If there's another way to accomplish your plans without sacrificing me, please do it!" Jesus finishes the prayer by accepting God's will, whatever it may be. That's the same principle Jesus included in his model prayer (Matthew 6:10).

MEDITATE:

MARK 14:38
Watch and pray so that you will not fall into temptation. The spirit is willing, but the flesh is weak.

DISCUSSION QUESTIONS:
THE PRAYERS OF JESUS

PURPOSE:
To review how Jesus prayed and wants us to pray.

QUESTIONS

1. What did you learn from Jesus' prayer life that is helpful for you personally?

2. How do you pray? When do you feel that your prayers are the most meaningful? Why?

3. What are the most challenging or meaningful parts of "The Lord's Prayer" (Luke 11:1-13)? Why?

4. When you pray, do you ever experience a sense of God's presence? Describe what it is like for you.

5. Have you ever prayed for God's help in a time when you were under great pressure? What happened? How has that experience changed your view of prayers? Of God?

6. Some people only pray when they have a problem or need something. How do you think God reacts to that? Do you ever pray for other things?

7. What are your biggest obstacles to prayer? How can you overcome these?

8. What could a "prayer lifestyle" look like? What are some practical ways you could remember to pray more?

OVERVIEW

THE ESSENTIAL JESUS YOUTH EDITION

THE HARD SAYINGS OF JESUS

Since you're pretty far along in our journey with Jesus, it's probably safe to assume that you've read some things that Jesus said that were helpful, interesting, and encouraging. I sure hope so! Jesus made some amazing statements that brought hope and joy and healing to people.

But, there are some other statements of Jesus that don't read as neat and tidy as some that we've already seen. For example, our next five readings look at some statements that Jesus made that were very difficult to understand. In fact, at one point, people were so turned off by his teaching that they said, "This is very hard to understand. How can anyone accept it?" and many left him (see John 6:60, NLT).

As you follow Jesus and study his words and teachings you'll find some words were soothing, some were scary, some were complex to understand, and some were difficult to obey. In our next five readings we'll look at these hard sayings of Jesus:

- "Whoever eats my flesh and drinks my blood has eternal life." What? That sounds gross.

- "Whoever blasphemes against the Holy Spirit will never be forgiven; he is guilty of an eternal sin." Never be forgiven—Really?

- "You may ask me for anything in my name, and I will do it." Anything? There's this really hot girl/guy that I'd like to be in relationship with—will Jesus do that one for me?

- "This is how my heavenly Father will treat each of you unless you forgive your brother from your heart." Forgiving others who have hurt us is tough to understand why and difficult to do.

- "If anyone would come after me, he must deny himself and take up his cross and follow me." The "follow me" part makes sense but what's the deal about taking up a cross?

There's definitely more than five difficult sayings of Jesus, but this is a good start. Read and think. If you're in a group, it might make for some interesting discussion. Regardless if you understand everything or not, know that Jesus loves you deeply.

71 SO BIZARRE!

PRAY IT:

Jesus, there are so many things I don't understand about You and Your ways, and now I'm looking at more "difficult sayings" in Your Word... Please help me understand. I want to know You more and I'm grateful for Your love letter—the Bible.

READ IT:

John 6:25-71

THINK ABOUT IT:

What thoughts typically go through your mind as you prepare to take communion?

TRY IT:

Break a piece of bread in pieces and eat them slowly. As you do, remember that Jesus is the bread of life whose body was broken on the cross for you.

WRITE IT:

Look up 1 Corinthians 7:31 and write this instructional verse here:

This is such a bizarre statement: "Whoever eats my flesh and drinks my blood has eternal life..." (54). No wonder the disciples were confused and offended (60-61). And it makes sense that the religious leaders were outraged. Plus, it's a disgusting image of eating human flesh—isn't that cannibalism? But, before you get too grossed out, realize that Jesus wasn't talking about physically eating his flesh and blood. Rather, he's talking about the spiritual connection that he has with his followers. Those who truly put their faith and trust in Jesus are united with God (57) and have eternal life (40). Today, we have an opportunity to reflect on this spiritual truth whenever we take communion. The bread and wine are reminders of the ultimate sacrifice of Jesus (broken body and spilled blood).

MEDITATE:

JOHN 6:35

Then Jesus declared, "I am the bread of life. Whoever comes to me will never go hungry, and whoever believes in me will never be thirsty."

72 A HOUSE DIVIDED

PRAY IT:
Jesus, speak clearly to me through Your Word. I'm so thankful that You forgive me and set me on the right path. I want to eat and drink from Your Word so I will live more like You.

READ IT:
Mark 3:20-35

THINK ABOUT IT:
If forgiveness is available to all, why do you think there is some sin that is unforgiveable?

TRY IT:
Spend a few minutes confessing your sins to God. Then spend some time thanking God for the forgiveness, love, and acceptance he offers through Jesus.

WRITE IT:
Make a list of the sins you've committed over the last week. After you finish making this list, write the word "Forgiven" in big, bold letters as a reminder of what is available because of Jesus.

The religious leaders were frustrated with Jesus; he'd been teaching, healing, and attracting big crowds (20). That's why they wanted to discredit him in the eyes of the public by accusing him of being possessed by demons (22). Jesus responds by telling a parable that easily destroys their false charge (23-27). His point about eternal sin was that by connecting the work of the Holy Spirit with demon possession, the religious leaders were turning away from God. While they continued in that posture, they would not be forgiven. The "unforgivable sin" is an on-going unwillingness to repent (turn to God) that prevents one from being forgiven.

MEDITATE:

MARK 3:28-29 (NLT)
Truly I tell you, people can be forgiven all their sins and every slander they utter, but whoever blasphemes against the Holy Spirit will never be forgiven; they are guilty of an eternal sin.

73 PRAYER GUARANTEE

PRAY IT:
"Praise be to God, who has not rejected my prayer or withheld his love from me!" (Psalm 66:20).

READ IT:
John 14:1-14

THINK ABOUT IT:
What results have you seen from your prayers? How has prayer changed you?

TRY IT:
See if you can pray about three things that will bring glory to the Father.

WRITE IT:
We often end our prayers "in Jesus' name." Write out what you think Jesus means by asking for something in his name.

Today's reading is part of a final coaching session Jesus had with his disciples (John 14-16). They're worried about all this "I'll be leaving" talk (1-5). Jesus reassures them in two ways: (1) he says they'll eventually be with him again (3), and (2) Jesus says they can ask for his help while they wait for his return (12-14). That promise applies all the way to today and to you, too. But the key to unlocking the mystery of Jesus' "prayer guarantee" lies in two phrases that are easy to overlook. The first is "in my name." When we pray, we should ask for things that are consistent with what Jesus taught and did. The second is "bring glory to the Father." When we pray, our focus should be on things that help more people understand who God really is. Those are the kind of prayers that get results.

MEDITATE:

JOHN 14:6
Jesus answered, "I am the way and the truth and the life. No one comes to the Father except through me."

74 SERIOUS FORGIVENESS

PRAY IT:
Jesus, thank You for showing me mercy when I didn't deserve it! I'm so thankful to You for forgiving my sin, even though I must ask Your forgiveness over and over again.

READ IT:
Matthew 18:15-35

THINK ABOUT IT:
Can you think of a time when you were in the wrong and someone forgave you? How did it make you feel?

TRY IT:
Who is someone in your life who you haven't forgiven? This is the person whose name triggers anger or hate. Forgive this person. First, talk to God. Second, write out your forgiveness (see "write it" assignment). Third, let the person know you have forgiven him/her.

WRITE IT:
Write out a letter of forgiveness to the person who you haven't forgiven. You may or may not want to share this letter with him/her... Regardless, it will be a good exercise for you to write it out.

Humans are experts at conflict and drama and tension. Relationships can be messy and Jesus gives teaching on this important issue. Today's Scripture involves conflict (15-20) and forgiveness—two biggies. Jesus doesn't support gossip—he says to first go to the person in private. If that doesn't work, go with others. Then, if it still doesn't work, involve the Church. Peter hears this and asks a sincere question about forgiveness. Peter wanted to know when he could stop forgiving someone. Basically Jesus says, "Keep forgiving" (that's "7 x 70"). Jesus wants us to understand that when we really appreciate how much God has forgiven us, we must forgive others. That sets up one of the most challenging statements Jesus ever made (35). The point of the parable (23-34) is that God is serious about forgiveness and if we want his forgiveness, we need to become serious about it too.

MEDITATE:

MATTHEW 18:21
Then Peter came to Jesus and asked, "Lord, how many times shall I forgive my brother or sister who sins against me? Up to seven times?" Jesus answered, "I tell you, not seven times, but seventy-seven times."

75 THIS IS SERIOUS!

PRAY IT:
Jesus, it's so easy to focus on the things of this world and so difficult to focus on the things that matter most to You. I want that to change in my life. I want to make the focus of my life a focus on You. Please help me to better see what is important to You.

READ IT:
Mark 8:31–9:1

THINK ABOUT IT:
What is typically the object of your focus?

TRY IT:
Find or make a cross and put it by your bathroom sink. Next, find something that reminds you of an earthly value (something you want/seek). It could be a coin, a dollar bill, a photo of a car you want, etc. Each morning, as you brush your teeth, look at those items as a reminder of the tension they create in your life. Ask yourself, "Which one am I going to pursue today?"

WRITE IT:
Write your response to this question: How will you "take up your cross" and follow Jesus today?

> This passage contains one of the most misunderstood statements Jesus ever made (34). You've probably seen people express their frustration and then complain, "Well, we all have our crosses to bear, don't we?" Jesus carrying his cross to death wasn't a simple frustration. For Jesus, taking up his cross was a symbol of all-out obedience to his Father's will. The cross meant giving up his rights as the Son of God (see Philippians 2:5-8) and dying for the sins of the world (see John 19:17-18). For followers of Jesus, this "follow me" requires us to focus our lives by living his way (35). We must "die" to our own plans and live for Jesus and his will for our lives. Ultimately, God's will is the only thing worth living for (35-36).

MEDITATE:

MARK 8:34
Then he called the crowd to him along with his disciples and said: "Whoever wants to be my disciple must deny themselves and take up their cross and follow me."

DISCUSSION QUESTIONS:
THE HARD SAYINGS OF JESUS

PURPOSE:
To review things that Jesus said that can be hard to live out.

QUESTIONS

1. Of all the things Jesus said (both in this section and elsewhere in the Gospels), which are the most difficult to understand? To obey? Why?

2. Was there ever a time in your life when you were running from God? What was it like?

3. What (or who) helps you feel closer to God? What (or who) pushes you away?

4. Have you ever experienced a specific answer to your prayers? What happened and did it change your relationship with God?

5. How do you resolve conflicts with people who have hurt or offended you?

6. Which is a bigger priority for you—pursuing happiness or following Jesus? Why?

7. Have you had to forgive or ask for forgiveness recently? Was it hard or easy to do? Why?

OVERVIEW

THE CRUCIFIXION OF JESUS

Jesus died on the cross and the crucifixion was awful and ugly. And yet the cross has become one of the most recognized symbols in the world. Jewelry, T-shirts, and tattoos are common places where you'll see this popular image. For some, the cross is nothing more than a design, while for others it has deep and significant meaning for their faith.

In our next five readings, we'll examine the Bible's account of the crucifixion of Jesus. The events that led to the death of Jesus were completely unfair and out of control; at least that's how it seemed from a human point of view. But even worse, crucifixion was perhaps the most horrible form of execution ever imagined—it was cruel and humiliating. Victims were stripped naked and whipped until their backs burst open, and they were forced to carry the wooden beams on which they would be hanged. Medical experts suggest that death could occur from any number of causes including shock to the body, loss of blood, or simply from suffocation from the hours or even days hanging there. Bottom line, it was a horrible way to die.

As you read, pay attention to the way Jesus reacted to his arrest, trials, and crucifixion. Though he was mistreated, he seems to be in control when his world was out of control. His death was no surprise—it's the reason he came to earth. He died so that all could have a real and eternal life.

What you're about to read isn't easy to digest, but it's essential for your faith to embrace. If you're reading this as part of a group, make sure you spend some time discussing what the crucifixion means for you.

76 THE KISS

PRAY IT:
Dear Jesus, even the thought of beginning to read, study, and reflect on the crucifixion makes me feel a little tense. I can't believe all You suffered for me. As I consume Your Word today may I get a deeper sense of Your love for me.

READ IT:
Matthew 26:47-56

THINK ABOUT IT:
Have you ever betrayed Jesus? If so, how?

TRY IT:
Unlike Judas, you have the opportunity to apologize and repent of your acts of betrayal. Spend some extended time in prayer and talk to Jesus about your actions and seek his forgiveness.

WRITE IT:
Write out your thoughts to this statement in verse 56: "Then all the disciples deserted him and fled." How does this make you feel?

We don't really know what motivated Judas to betray Jesus. But we do know that his betrayal was intentional. Judas planned exactly how he would do it (48-49). What's incredible with this event is that in the midst of all that was happening Jesus still had enough love to call Judas his "friend" (50). Jesus was calm. He was confident. And, he was in control. Jesus could have easily stopped Judas and the gang of thugs in a second with a heavenly army (53), but he allows himself to be arrested without a fight (56). That's because Jesus' highest priority wasn't to save himself—it was to fulfill the mission God had given him (54, 56). Thank you, Jesus!

MEDITATE:

MATTHEW 26:52-53
"Put your sword back in its place," Jesus said to him, "for all who draw the sword will die by the sword. Do you think I cannot call on my Father, and he will at once put at my disposal more than twelve legions of angels?"

77 CRAZY COURT

PRAY IT:
Jesus, thank You for Your sacrificial love. You did everything for me to have a relationship with You and I've done nothing. I need You and am so grateful that You love me and want me close to You.

READ IT:
Matthew 26:57-68

THINK ABOUT IT:
What do you think motivated the two men to come forward and speak against Jesus?

TRY IT:
Engage with a person who has rejected Jesus. Be gracious and kind, but ask him/her the simple question: "I'm trying to learn why people reject Jesus. Would you mind telling me why you've chosen to refuse him?"

WRITE IT:
Write out two or three popular "charges" people bring against Jesus today. Then, try to write a sentence defending Jesus against each one.

Jesus was at the mercy of this Sanhedrin court. Caiaphas and the group of high priests and religious leaders were looking for anything against Jesus and they broke all the rules of a fair trial. It was a horrible, no-win trial for Jesus. First, the trial took place at night instead of during the day. Second, the charges were based on false evidence and false witnesses (59-60). And the judge and jury had already made up their minds to execute Jesus (59). They felt like they had all the needed evidence: Jesus claimed to be the Son of God (63-65). Caiaphas rightly identified that as the central issue, but he was unwilling to accept Jesus on that basis. That's the biggest mistake anyone can ever make with Jesus.

MEDITATE:

MATTHEW 26:63-64
The high priest said to him, "I charge you under oath by the living God: Tell us if you are the Messiah, the Son of God." "You have said so," Jesus replied. "But I say to all of you: From now on you will see the Son of Man sitting at the right hand of the Mighty One and coming on the clouds of heaven."

78 PETER & THE ROOSTER

PRAY IT:
"Our God, you bless everyone whose sins you forgive and wipe away. You bless them by saying, 'You told me your sins, without trying to hide them, and now I forgive you'" (Psalm 32:1-2, CEV).

READ IT:
Matthew 26:69–27:10

THINK ABOUT IT:
What are some ways in which you have denied Jesus?

TRY IT:
Do or say something today that makes it clear that you are a follower of Jesus. If you receive any pressure or mocking, how did it make you feel?

WRITE IT:
List three situations in which you feel pressured to either deny Jesus or keep quiet about him. How does it make you feel to write them and bring them out in the open?

Reading about Peter's denial of Jesus feels like an autobiography—most people have a similar experience of some type of denial. Peter's denial leads to his heart breaking and deep crying (26:75). His denial also leads to a stronger faith (as we'll see in a future reading: John 21:15-19). If we are willing to repent of the ways we deny Jesus and sin against him, no failure is so great that it will separate us from God (Romans 8:28-39). Tragically, Judas never understood that. Although he felt deep remorse (27:3) and recognized his sin (27:4), it doesn't appear that he repented. There would have been hope for him even at this final hour. Like the thief on the cross, Judas could have called out to Jesus (Luke 23:39-43) and been forgiven.

MEDITATE:

MATTHEW 26:74
Then he began to call down curses, and he swore to them, "I don't know the man!" Immediately a rooster crowed. Then Peter remembered the word Jesus had spoken: "Before the rooster crows, you will disown me three times." And he went outside and wept bitterly.

79 POLITICAL PRESSURE

PRAY IT:
Jesus, I understand why the Bible challenges me to "remember" so often... I am great at forgetting. I forget about Your love, Your presence, Your power... As I focus on Your Word today, may I be reminded of Your greatness.

READ IT:
Luke 22:66–23:25

THINK ABOUT IT:
Why do you think Pilate gave in to Jesus' enemies? Do you think modern politicians feel pressures from people to do the wrong thing?

TRY IT:
Barabbas seems to be one lucky guy. Take a minute and read a little more about him (http://en.wikipedia.org/wiki/Barabbas).

WRITE IT:
If someone were to ask you, "Tell us, is Jesus the Messiah?" what would you say? Write down your response.

Our passage gives us two examples of religion and politics getting messy. Herod was interested in Jesus, but only for his own entertainment (23:8). It's not unusual for politicians to want to draw near to those who are popular. But Jesus made it clear that he was not interested in entertaining a politician (23:9). Jesus didn't come to play any role other than Savior. The other politician, Pilate, is caught in the tension of the moment. Part of him wants to do the right thing (23:13-17, 20-22) but in the end he didn't believe there was any such thing as truth (see John 18:38) and it caused him to reject the ultimate source of Truth.

MEDITATE:

LUKE 22:70
They all asked, "Are you then the Son of God?" He replied, "You say that I am."

80 REMEMBER ME

PRAY IT:
"Remember not the sins of my youth and my rebellious ways; according to your love remember me, for you are good, O LORD" (Psalm 25:7, KJV).

READ IT:
Luke 23:26-56

THINK ABOUT IT:
Take time to put yourself in this story. What do you think and feel as you imagine yourself at the foot of the cross?

TRY IT:
Spend a few minutes humbly thanking Jesus for what he went through for you on the cross.

WRITE IT:
Respond to this statement:
"Because of what Jesus did on the cross I..."

It's difficult to read this passage without feeling like you're on holy ground. The crucifixion of Jesus is the most amazing demonstration of sacrificial love the world has ever seen. We will never fully know the extent of the suffering Jesus went through so that we could be forgiven of our sins and restored to God. This passage offers us the very picture of why Jesus came... To die... For us. Because of our sin we're like one of the two thieves—We'll either respond to Jesus with insults and anger (39) or with a heartfelt "remember me" (42).

MEDITATE:

LUKE 23:41-43
"We are punished justly, for we are getting what our deeds deserve. But this man has done nothing wrong." Then he said, "Jesus, remember me when you come into your kingdom." Jesus answered him, "Truly I tell you, today you will be with me in paradise."

DISCUSSION QUESTIONS:
THE CRUCIFIXION OF JESUS

PURPOSE:
To review what loyalty to Jesus looks like and why he was crucified.

QUESTIONS

1. Have you ever known someone who has completely turned away from Jesus? Do you know why they made that choice?

2. What factors or situations in your life make you want to deny Jesus?

3. Do you think some people can become so bad or evil that they lose the opportunity to return to Jesus? Do you think Judas had a chance to change his mind?

4. Have you ever hidden your identity as a follower of Jesus? If so, explain the situation. Have you ever been bold about your faith at a time when you felt pressure to hide it? What happened and how did you feel afterwards?

5. At Jesus' trial, some people obviously hated him. Do you know anyone who hates Jesus? What do you think motivates them to feel like this?

6. How would you explain the crucifixion to a person who has never heard of Jesus?

7. What difference has Jesus' death made in your life? What difference could his sacrifice make for you personally?

THE RESURRECTION OF JESUS

Most schools have something called "Open House." It usually happens at the beginning of the school year for all parents to meet the teachers and get the big-picture view of what's about to happen. For those of us who work in the church, we often view our "open house" seasons as Christmas and Easter. Obviously people can attend church every week, but many will only attend during these two special holidays. Because of that reality, just about everyone knows the two stories connected with Christmas (the birth of Jesus) and Easter (Jesus' resurrection).

In the next five readings we'll look closely at the resurrection from the four different Gospel writers' point of view. Each writer captured unique details and viewpoints of what happened.

- Matthew expresses his view by linking the experiences of four separate people together.

- Mark emphasizes the power that was revealed by the resurrection.

- Luke adds an interesting encounter that two disciples had with the resurrected Jesus.

- John highlights the relationship between Peter and Jesus after the resurrection.

When we read all these different perspectives we get a more complete picture of what actually happened.

In our fifth reading, we'll look at what the Apostle Paul taught about the resurrection many years later. As years passed, Christians were beginning to entertain doubts about whether the resurrection of Jesus ever really happened. So Paul wrote to reassure them and express the importance of the historical, factual, "yes it did happen" resurrection.

Whether you're reading this as an individual or discussing this as a group, as you go through these readings, be praying that God will enhance your faith as you think deeply about the power of God expressed through the resurrection of Jesus.

81 THE EMPTY TOMB

PRAY IT:
Jesus, I want to "come and see" for myself what happened in that tomb. Please give me new insights into the truth about Your resurrection as I read Your Word and reflect on Your greatness.

READ IT:
Matthew 28:1-20

THINK ABOUT IT:
If you were one of the first followers of Jesus, what would scare you about the empty tomb?

TRY IT:
Pause for an extra minute today and give God praise for defeating death. The resurrection of Jesus is the game-changer to our faith—everything rests on the resurrection of Jesus (see 1 Corinthians 15:12-14).

WRITE IT:
Write down your top 3 fears to the thought of "going and telling" the good news of Jesus. Who is someone you can share these fears with? Write that person's name down too.

The two women are overwhelmed with conflicting emotions, fear and joy (8). Even so, the angel gives them a threefold command: "Don't be afraid" (5), "Come and see" (6), and "Go and tell" (7). Those are good instructions for any follower of Jesus. The latter verses within today's reading (16-20) are often given the title "The Great Commission" because this is where Jesus empowers his followers to share the good news of the gospel with the whole world—this would be the "go and tell" part of the command. Whether that command scares you or excites you, you can be assured that Jesus will be with his followers forever (20).

MEDITATE:

MATTHEW 28:19-20
Therefore go and make disciples of all nations, baptizing them in the name of the Father and of the Son and of the Holy Spirit, and teaching them to obey everything I have commanded you. And surely I am with you always, to the very end of the age.

82 THAT'S SOME POWER!

PRAY IT:
Jesus, I want to know and experience more of the power of the resurrection. Please reveal more of Yourself to me as I read Your Word.

READ IT:
Mark 16:1-20

THINK ABOUT IT:
What is the most powerful thing about the resurrection of Jesus to you? Why?

TRY IT:
Find some type of power switch in your house (i.e., TV, microwave, oven, etc...). Every time you walk past that power switch say, "Thank you, Jesus, for defeating death with Your power."

WRITE IT:
The gospel has the power to change lives. How has God's Word changed your life? Write out 3 ways your life has been changed.

Some Bibles include a note that says "[The earliest manuscripts and some other ancient witnesses do not have verses 9–20.]" You might be thinking, "What's the deal with that?" Scholars have offered different explanations, but the most likely is that either Mark died just before he finished his Gospel account, or that the last section of his writing scroll was somehow destroyed. Some believe someone close to Mark filled in the last section. We'll never know for sure, but over the centuries the church has agreed that these verses are still part of the inspired Word of God.

MEDITATE:

MARK 16:19-20
After the Lord Jesus had spoken to them, he was taken up into heaven and he sat at the right hand of God. Then the disciples went out and preached everywhere, and the Lord worked with them and confirmed his word by the signs that accompanied it.

83 THE THIRD WALKER

PRAY IT:
There is so much I want to learn about You, Jesus. Oftentimes I miss You in the ordinary parts of my day. There are times when I walk through my day and don't even consider that You're there. Forgive me. Help me to see that You're with me.

READ IT:
Luke 24:1-49

THINK ABOUT IT:
When you read about the walk to Emmaus, there seemed to be confusion about Jesus. What do you think is the most common confusion among your friends today?

TRY IT:
Go for a short walk and think through what you read from verses 13-49. As you're walking, imagine walking next to Jesus. Talk to him as you walk.

WRITE IT:
Today's reading is the third account in the third different Gospel (see days 81-82). Go back through those other readings (Matthew 28:1-20 and Mark 16:1-20) and write down the key verses that are the most powerful or helpful to you in believing in Jesus' resurrection. Consider keeping them in a place where you can review them regularly.

It's so easy to make fun of these two guys for not recognizing Jesus. We don't fully know why... if they were too focused on their own pain or if it was because God's Spirit didn't want them to fully see Jesus in that moment. But, regardless of why it happened, it was a life-changing walk with Jesus. Wouldn't you love to have been part of that small, private walk with Jesus? Well, in a sense, you are. As you follow Jesus and discover for yourself "what was said in all the Scriptures" (27) about the essential Jesus, it's as if you are "the third disciple" on the road to Emmaus. Our prayer would be that you'd come to the same conclusion as the others: "It's true!" (34).

MEDITATE:

LUKE 24:5B-7
"Why do you look for the living among the dead? He is not here; he has risen! Remember how he told you, while he was still with you in Galilee: 'The Son of Man must be delivered over to the hands of sinners, be crucified and on the third day be raised again.'"

84 FOLLOW ME

PRAY IT:

I want to follow You, Jesus. Not just to church or youth group, I want to follow Your ways, Your thoughts, Your commands... I want to be a follower of You in all areas of my life. I fall so short. Forgive me. Now guide me through Your Word today.

READ IT:

John 20:1–21:25

THINK ABOUT IT:

Which of the four characters in this passage do you identify with the most? Mary? Thomas? Peter? John? Why?

TRY IT:

There is so much happening in this longer Scripture reading. Slowly go back through today's reading to find one verse that really "pops out" at you. Read over that verse several times and pray, "Jesus, what are you trying to say to me?"

WRITE IT:

Thomas had doubts and questions. Write the biggest doubt or question you have. Who is someone you could pursue who might help you answer it?

John's account of the resurrection seems to focus on how different people reacted to it. Mary Magdalene had been cured of demon possession by Jesus (Mark 16:9, Luke 8:2). She was the first one to the tomb. Others had questions about Jesus' resurrection (20:9), but Thomas was the only one with the guts to admit that his question and/or doubts were real (20:28). Peter had failed Jesus and must re-affirm his love for him. It's clear John has developed a special relationship with Jesus and a firm belief in the truth of his resurrection (20:8). There's a lot happening here. How would you be described as a follower of Jesus?

MEDITATE:

JOHN 21:25

Jesus did many other things as well. If every one of them were written down, I suppose that even the whole world would not have room for the books that would be written.

85 WHERE'S THE EVIDENCE?

PRAY IT:
Thank You, Jesus, that death is not the end of life... rather just a change. Thank You for the power of the resurrection and the hope it gives me today.

READ IT:
1 Corinthians 15:1-58

THINK ABOUT IT:
Why is the fact of Christ's actual, literal resurrection so important?

TRY IT:
Approach a friend who is a follower of Jesus and ask him/her what difference the resurrection of Jesus makes to him/her today.

WRITE IT:
In your own words, paraphrase verses 55-56. After you rewrite them, write out what they mean to you.

It had been several years since Jesus lived, and people were beginning to ask tough questions: Did his resurrection actually happen? And if it did, what significance does it have for us now? When you think about it, these are the same questions people have today. So how did Paul answer? He starts by giving his account of the resurrection (verses 3-8), and although Paul didn't go to the empty tomb himself that morning, he did have an encounter with the resurrected Jesus some time later (Acts 9:1-19). He also had another reliable source of information, one that is still available to us today: he studied the Scriptures (verses 3-4). That's the best way to answer our questions about Jesus.

MEDITATE:

1 CORINTHIANS 15:14
And if Christ has not been raised, our preaching is useless and so is your faith.

DISCUSSION QUESTIONS:
THE RESURRECTION OF JESUS

PURPOSE:
To discuss the main events of Jesus' resurrection.

QUESTIONS

1. How would you respond to someone who said, "You can still be a good Christian and not believe that Jesus was literally raised from the dead. It just doesn't square with what we know about science today."?

2. How would you explain the importance of the resurrection to someone?

3. Have you ever had a misunderstanding about something in the Bible? What was it and what could you do to find answers?

4. Based on Jesus' response to Peter, how should we respond to others who fail?

5. What are the most important things to being a follower of Jesus? Are your ideas different from Peter's and John's?

6. How do you share the good news about Jesus in your world?

7. If you could determine how Christians fulfill the Great Commission, who would you start with? What would you do and why?

OVERVIEW

THE EARLY CHURCH OF JESUS

Our next set of readings takes us into the wild and difficult-to-understand Book of Revelation. This book records a vision that the Apostle John had nearly 60 years after the death and resurrection of Jesus. In his vision, it's as if Jesus were visiting seven different churches and then making unique comments on each of them.

Of the seven churches mentioned in Revelation, five of them fall into a "good news/bad news" category: Jesus praises them for some things and then scolds them for other things. Only two of the churches fall into an "all good" category and Jesus praises them in spite of the fact that they are both facing severe struggles.

As you'll discover, some of the details in the Book of Revelation are challenging to understand. That's partly because it's a written record of a vision or a dream. But even though it's hard to understand, the main point of the next five readings is this: Jesus knows what's going on in the Church and he really, really cares. So let's get going and see if we can piece together what Jesus thinks is so important for the Church to understand. And, by the way, for those of you meeting in a group, you are the Church—by meeting and caring for one another.

86 A VISION

PRAY IT:
I'm so easily confused by what I read in Your Word, Jesus, and I'm a little nervous as I begin to look for You in the next several readings. Please give me a wisdom and insight that is greater than my own.

READ IT:
Revelation 1:1-20

THINK ABOUT IT:
John shares his vision here. What does it teach you about Jesus? How does it change or help your concept of Jesus?

TRY IT:
Make a list of the major characteristics of Jesus that you found in this passage. Try to commit one of them to memory over the next week.

WRITE IT:
What "message" might Jesus have for you and your church? Write it here.

People often call this last book of the Bible "John's Revelation." But a better title, based on the opening sentence, would be "The Revelation of Jesus Christ" (1). As we begin our exploration of this challenging book, it's important to understand that although the Apostle John recorded this incredible vision, the Book of Revelation is all about Jesus. And right away we'll notice the consistency between John's view and the rest of the New Testament. Jesus is "the first born from the dead" (5, see Colossians 1:15, 18); he has freed us from sin "by his blood" (5b, see Romans 5:9 and Ephesians 1:7); his followers are "a kingdom and priests" (6, see 1 Peter 2:9); and someday Jesus will come again and "every eye will see him" (7, see Philippians 2:9-11).

MEDITATE:

REVELATION 1:8
"I am the Alpha and the Omega," says the Lord God, "who is, and who was, and who is to come, the Almighty."

THE EARLY CHURCH OF JESUS

87 YOUR FIRST LOVE

PRAY IT:
The thought of falling out of love with You, Jesus... It just hurts my soul. I want to express my love for You in how I think and how I live. May my heart turned toward Your Word be a reflection of what is in my heart.

READ IT:
Revelation 2:1-11

THINK ABOUT IT:
In what ways might you be criticized for "forsaking your first love" of Jesus?

TRY IT:
Fill in the blank with the Bible verse where these statements are found in verses 2-6:
1. Work hard for the gospel (verse ____).
2. Hate/avoid false teaching (verse ____ & verse ____).
3. Persevere in faith under hardship (verse ____).
4. Keep your love for Jesus aflame (verse ____).
5. Be willing and ready to repent when necessary (verse ____).

WRITE IT:
Write out what it means for one to repent. If you don't know, look up the word or check out a commentary for verses 4-5.

Here, we read Jesus' assessment of the churches in the First Century. The first one was in the city of Ephesus (1-7). The good news is that they were activists; they were willing to work hard (2). The bad news was they'd forsaken their first love, Jesus (4). The way to rekindle dying love is to repent and start over again (5). The second church, Smyrna (8-11), was one of two that were singled out for commendation only (the other is in Philadelphia, 3:7-14). They were poor, were being criticized, and their members were about to suffer persecution and imprisonment (8-10).

MEDITATE:

REVELATION 2:4-5A
Yet I hold this against you: You have forsaken the love you had at first. Consider how far you have fallen! Repent and do the things you did at first.

88 "HOLD ON... UNTIL I RETURN."

PRAY IT:
I want to walk more closely to You today, Jesus. I want to find a rhythm of my life where it's so natural to connect and communicate with You. Open my eyes to see what You'd have for me today.

READ IT:
Revelation 2:12-29

THINK ABOUT IT:
What do you think would be the warning to today's Church?

TRY IT:
Ask someone who is older than you (parent, friend, youth pastor) to give you an idea of what some of the problems or issues have been with the Church in the last decade.

WRITE IT:
Make a list of what seems praiseworthy about these two churches. Do you see these same qualities in the church you attend?

There are no perfect churches because churches are made up of imperfect people. In the midst of the issues, it's vital to be part of a church who loves and follows Jesus and teaches truth. The two churches from this reading had problems just like today's church. The church at Pergamum (12-17) had remained true to Jesus during unusual stress and persecution (13). But that spiritual victory was long past; now they were being misdirected by false teaching (14-15). The church in Thyatira was also accepting false teaching that was leading to bad behavior (20). Since there's no perfect church we've got to hang on to Jesus' words, "Hold on to what you have until I come" (25). In other words, remain faithful to God's Word with anticipation of Jesus' return.

MEDITATE:

REVELATION 2:9
I know your deeds, your love and faith, your service and perseverance, and that you are now doing more than you did at first.

89 CHURCH—DEAD OR ALIVE?

PRAY IT:
Jesus, give me the wisdom to see beyond the surface of life. There are many things that look good (even churches) that may not be right for me. I need Your help in better understanding what's beyond the surface. Please grant me Your wisdom today.

READ IT:
Revelation 3:1-13

THINK ABOUT IT:
Do you think Jesus would consider your church dead or alive? Why?

TRY IT:
Take an old plant or branch or something that used to be alive and set it by your bathroom sink for a week. Allow it to remind you that water can keep plants from dying. Think about the "spiritual water" you need every day to keep you alive spiritually.

WRITE IT:
In your opinion, what are some qualities of an "alive" church? Write them down and then consider those qualities in comparison to the church you attend.

There may be churches in your neighborhood that appear to be alive and healthy, but their appearance may not indicate their spiritual health. Just because a church is large and "drawing a crowd" doesn't mean the people are following Jesus. In today's reading, the church in Sardis (1-6) had "a reputation of being alive" (verse 1), but Jesus considered it dead (1b) because the members weren't obeying the basic teachings of the gospel (2-3). But the other church in Philadelphia was worthy of praise and compliments (7-13). Like the church at Smyrna, it didn't look successful because they were weak and facing opposition (8-9), but they got the main things right... they kept the Word of God (8). Whether you are currently in "a dead church" or one that is "alive," Jesus says you will "walk with me" if you remain faithful to him and his Word (4).

MEDITATE:

REVELATION 3:2-3
Wake up! Strengthen what remains and is about to die, for I have found your deeds unfinished in the sight of my God. Remember, therefore, what you have received and heard; hold it fast, and repent. But if you do not wake up, I will come like a thief, and you will not know at what time I will come to you.

90 THE PASSIONLESS OF BEING LUKEWARM

PRAY IT:
Jesus, You know my "spiritual temperature" even better than I do. Where I'm lukewarm, I pray that You'll help me develop a real passion for You.

READ IT:
Revelation 3:14-22

THINK ABOUT IT:
How would you characterize your relationship with Jesus right now—on fire, on ice, or lukewarm? Why?

TRY IT:
Pick one way you can show others that you're passionate for God this week. This is not an exercise to be weird or an extremist... It's a challenge to be thoughtful and extend your love for Jesus to others.

WRITE IT:
If a friend's relationship with Jesus is "lukewarm," how would you encourage him/her to recover their passion for Jesus? Write your response:

Passion is exciting! People want to follow those who are passionate and have a sense about themselves that they know what is important. "Lukewarm" doesn't communicate that passion. Lukewarm isn't attractive... it's blah. No one would ever accuse the church in Laodicea of being passionate about God (14-22). Their being lukewarm really bothered Jesus (15-16). It's safe to assume that "lukewarm" is still a turn-off to Jesus. For the Laodiceans, it was their wealth that had cooled their passion toward the things of God (17). Money isn't bad (see 1 Timothy 6:10, the "love of money" is bad), but it's impossible to love both God and money (see Matthew 6:24).

MEDITATE:

REVELATION 3:15-16
I know your deeds, that you are neither cold nor hot. I wish you were either one or the other! So, because you are lukewarm—neither hot nor cold—I am about to spit you out of my mouth.

DISCUSSION QUESTIONS:
THE EARLY CHURCH OF JESUS

PURPOSE:
To review what the early church was like and compare it to our own churches.

QUESTIONS

1. If Jesus visited your church, do you think he'd like it? What message do you think he would have for your church?

2. How can we be faithful in peace and prosperity?

3. How can a person who has it "all together" keep Jesus as his/her first love?

4. Do you think Christians today have become "too tolerant" or "too extreme"? Of what? Why?

5. Have you ever felt distant from or uncaring about God? How could you tell? What did you do about it?

6. Have you ever been in a church that seemed distant from or uncaring about God?

7. Is there any way you can help your church "stay awake" and faithful?

OVERVIEW

THE SECOND COMING OF JESUS

The Bible tells us that as Jesus was ascending into heaven, after his death and resurrection, two angels appeared to the disciples and said, "This same Jesus, who has been taken from you into heaven, will come back in the same way you have seen him go into heaven" (Acts 1:11). Ever since then, for 2,000 plus years, the idea of a "second coming" of Jesus has been eagerly anticipated by those of us who follow Jesus.

Our next five readings will help us better understand what the Bible says about Jesus' Second Coming. First, we'll examine his ascension—that means him leaving earth and going to heaven. Understanding the ascension will be a "preview" of what his second coming will actually be like. Then we'll consider the teachings of two key leaders in the early church—Paul and Peter. And finally, we'll study Revelation 21–22 to get a better picture of what the end times will be like.

The encouraging thing about all that you'll read is that even though these readings describe the end, it's really only the beginning. It's the beginning of a new world with God at its center.

The Bible makes the Second Coming pretty clear, but many still seem confused about it. Some people make too much of it and their worldview is built around some weird, minor detail surrounding the end times. They overemphasize what wasn't meant to be overemphasized. Others make too little of the Second Coming; for them, it might or might not happen, but who cares?

Our goal will be to form a balanced, biblical view of the Second Coming, because someday Jesus will come back in the same way that he went up into heaven... and what an amazing day that will be!

91 THE GREATEST SEQUEL OF ALL TIME

PRAY IT:
If I'm being really honest, Jesus, it's difficult to totally understand this idea of "a second coming." I am committed to reading Your Word and learning, and I beg You to give me a depth of insight that is so much stronger than my own about Your eventual return.

READ IT:
Acts 1:1-11

THINK ABOUT IT:
If you knew Jesus was returning within the week, what difference would it make for how you live your life?

TRY IT:
According to verse 3, Jesus gave his followers "many convincing truths" over 40 days before he ascended. Go back through the Gospels and make a list of some of those truths.

WRITE IT:
If you had to give a title to today's reading, what would it be? Write your title here:

Have you ever seen a movie where the ending leaves you with that strong feeling that it's not over? A Part 2 is called "a sequel." In a sense, that's exactly what's happening in this passage. Luke, the writer of Acts, is setting up the greatest sequel of all time—he's preparing us for the Second Coming of Jesus Christ. He does it by describing Jesus' last moments on earth. Luke had finished his Gospel account with a reference to the ascension of Jesus (see Luke 24:50-53), but here he gives a fuller description of that unforgettable event. As Jesus disappears into the clouds, it is the two angels who have the privilege of announcing the great sequel. Jesus "will come back in the same way you have seen him go into heaven" (11). Just imagine how unbelievable that would be if it happened during your lifetime!

MEDITATE:

ACTS 1:8
But you will receive power when the Holy Spirit comes on you; and you will be my witnesses in Jerusalem, and in all Judea and Samaria, and to the ends of the earth.

92 WHAT DAY WILL JESUS RETURN?

PRAY IT:
The more I read about You, Jesus, and think about Your ways, the more I'm drawn to You. I love You and want to follow You. Lead me to deeper places today as I read and think about Your Word.

READ IT:
1 Thessalonians 4:13–5:11

THINK ABOUT IT:
Are you ready for Jesus to return? Why or why not?

TRY IT:
Ask a fellow follower of Jesus what he/she is looking forward to about eternal life.

WRITE IT:
Write out what you would want said about you at your funeral. Why might this type of thinking (thinking about death) be helpful to really live?

People throughout the ages have been interested as to what happens to them after they die. The Apostle Paul explains to the Thessalonian church how they need to have a calm, balanced understanding of the Second Coming. First they shouldn't spend time trying to figure out the exact "times and dates" of Jesus' return (5:1). Jesus told us that only God knows when it will happen (see Matthew 24:36). If we're not prepared, Jesus' return will take us by surprise (5:2). The second thing Paul teaches is that they should spend time trying to live for God in the present (5:4-8). It's okay to be interested and curious about the Second Coming, but it's more important to be ready for it.

MEDITATE:

1 THESSALONIANS 5:1-2
Now, brothers and sisters, about times and dates we do not need to write to you, for you know very well that the day of the Lord will come like a thief in the night.

93 DON'T BE ALARMED

PRAY IT:
Jesus, help me see You, Your big picture, and Your plans for my life more clearly today.

READ IT:
2 Thessalonians 2:1-12

THINK ABOUT IT:
What do you believe the Second Coming will be like?

TRY IT:
When your alarm clock goes off tomorrow, think or say to yourself, "Nothing will alarm me today. Jesus is in control."

WRITE IT:
Based on today's reading, how would you respond to this quote: "Don't worry about the Second Coming. God will take care of it—and you." Write your thoughts... Do you agree? Disagree?

Today's reading gives us another puzzle piece that helps us better understand the mystery of the Second Coming. It appears as though there was a lot of misinformation being spread, and as a result, many believers worried they had been left behind (2). The Apostle Paul doesn't want them to be deceived (3), and simply reminds them of the basics: when Jesus returns, his followers will be with him (1). In other words, when it happens, you'll know. Paul also reveals some kind of "rebellion" and the appearance of "the man of lawlessness" (3). During the final conflict between God and Satan, a key instrument of Satan called "the Antichrist" will oppose God and be defeated (see Matthew 24:1-51, Mark 13:1-37, Revelation 19:19-21; 20:7-10). So what does all this mean for us today? Since we already know the end of the story (Jesus wins)... Don't be alarmed... Be ready.

MEDITATE:

2 THESSALONIANS 2:2
[Don't] become easily unsettled or alarmed by the teaching allegedly from us—whether by a prophecy or by word of mouth or by letter—asserting that the day of the Lord has already come.

94 WHILE YOU'RE WAITING

PRAY IT:
Jesus, I want to have an eager spirit that anticipates Your return. I want to walk so closely to You that when I eventually see You... I will know You.

READ IT:
2 Peter 3:1-18

THINK ABOUT IT:
Do you ever have doubts about the Second Coming of Jesus? What are they and what helps you overcome them?

TRY IT:
In *The Message* paraphrase, verse 9 says, "He is restraining himself on account of you, holding back the End because he doesn't want anyone lost. He's giving everyone space and time to change." Make a list of three people in your life who you know are [spiritually] lost. Begin to pray for them.

WRITE IT:
Write your response to this: "The delay of Jesus' return is an example of God's grace" (9, 15).

First-century Christians were waiting for the Second Coming but nothing was happening. Skeptics were becoming more vocal with their criticisms (4). Peter points to the words of the prophets and the words of Jesus himself (2). He reminds his readers that when God speaks, things happen. And since God's Word says the Second Coming will happen, we can be sure it will (7). Second, God is outside of time and doesn't sit around marking his calendar like we do (8). What seems like a long delay is actually an opportunity for more people to come to know him (15). While we wait for the return of Jesus, we can focus on living "holy and godly lives" (11). Then we'll be drawing closer and closer to Jesus while we wait for that day when we meet him face to face (see 1 Corinthians 13:12). What a day that will be!

MEDITATE:

2 PETER 3:8-9
But do not forget this one thing, dear friends: With the Lord a day is like a thousand years, and a thousand years are like a day. The Lord is not slow in keeping his promise, as some understand slowness. Instead he is patient with you, not wanting anyone to perish, but everyone to come to repentance.

95 ALL THINGS NEW

PRAY IT:

Thank You for giving me new life, Jesus. I am a new creation because of Your love for me. I celebrate that truth today as I approach Your Word.

READ IT:

Revelation 21:1–22:21

THINK ABOUT IT:

Should God's plan to establish a new heaven and a new earth affect the way we live right now?

TRY IT:

If you've got something around your house that's new, look at it closely. Let it remind you of God's promise to one day make all things new.

WRITE IT:

Write out a list of the broken parts of the world that you look forward to being made new.

There are probably a few things about this passage, as well as the entire book of Revelation, that you may have found difficult to follow. It's important to remember that Revelation is the record of a vision, therefore it's best to focus on the main, big-picture points rather than every little detail. The main point in these last two chapters is that God intends to establish "a new heaven and a new earth" (21:1). Satan will be defeated (20:7-10), the curse of sin will be broken (22:3), and God the Father and God the Son will be present with us ("God's home is now among his people! He will live with them, and they will be his people. God himself will be with them" 21:3, NLT). For those who belong to Jesus, the end of the world is only the beginning of eternal life with Jesus (see Romans 6:23).

MEDITATE:

REVELATION 21:6-7

He said to me: "It is done. I am the Alpha and the Omega, the Beginning and the End. To the thirsty I will give water without cost from the spring of the water of life. Those who are victorious will inherit all this, and I will be their God and they will be my children."

DISCUSSION QUESTIONS:
THE SECOND COMING OF JESUS

PURPOSE:
To review why the Second Coming of Jesus is important to our faith.

QUESTIONS

1. How do you feel about the state of the world today? Does it seem worse, better, or the same as it's always been? Why?

2. How would you respond to a friend who says, "Look, after 2,000 years I think it's safe to assume that Jesus isn't going to come back." Could Jesus have meant it more as a figure of speech rather than an actual promise to return? Does it really matter? Why or why not?

3. Why would we make things better in the here and now, if God is just going to create a new heaven and a new earth anyway?

4. Some Christians say that since Jesus is coming back, evangelism is the most important thing and that we shouldn't waste too much time on things like peace, justice, poverty, and the environment. What do you say?

5. What do you think heaven will be like? Who will be there and how can you be sure that you will be one of them?

6. In what ways does the Second Coming of Jesus affect the way you live in your everyday life?

7. If you knew Jesus was coming back in 30 days, would that change the choices you make?

OVERVIEW

WHO IS JESUS... TO YOU?

Congratulations! You've done an amazing job at staying committed to this journey. Way to go! In this final set of readings (can you believe it's the last set of readings?), you'll have an opportunity to examine the experiences of five people who had significant encounters with Jesus: (1) The rich young man, who walked away from Jesus because he loved his money too much to part with it. (2) Nicodemus, who didn't believe Jesus at first, but over time became his follower. (3) The woman at the well, who had to face her shame and then got so excited about Jesus that she invited the whole town to see the person who changed her life. (4) Saul, who had a dramatic encounter with Jesus that changed his life, and the world, forever. And finally, (5) Peter, who made a stunning statement about Jesus even though he didn't fully understand all that it would cost him.

The theme that weaves through all these readings is that each of these five individuals had to make a personal decision about Jesus.

The reason we want to end here is because there's one more story you'll need to seriously consider before closing this book: yours! We want you to think deeply about your personal story with Jesus. When you finish the 100th reading it would be wise to spend some time reflecting on all you've read. If you're going through this as a group, share about your individual journey with Jesus. As you reflect on what you've read, imagine that Jesus is with you and lovingly asking you, "Who do you say I am?" How do you answer? Talk to Jesus and openly share what's on your heart.

Again, congratulations on completing 100 readings! That's amazing! But don't let this be the end of your times in God's Word. Our prayer is that it becomes the beginning of a lifetime of meeting with Jesus every day in the Bible and through prayerful conversations.

96 CAN'T EARN YOUR SALVATION

PRAY IT:
Jesus, help me to follow You to the places where I'm most scared. There are some things I want to hold on to that I know are keeping me from faithfully following You. I need Your help.

READ IT:
Matthew 19:16-30

THINK ABOUT IT:
Do you really think this young man had kept all the commandments? (See verse 19.) Why would that be important?

TRY IT:
Make a list of the things that are most important to you right now. Do the items on the list get in the way of you being a fully devoted follower of Jesus?

WRITE IT:
Rewrite verse 23 without using the camel metaphor. Put that verse in today's language. How would you describe the radical nature that Jesus communicates with camel/eye of the needle language?

So many people want the answer to this very old question: "How do I get to heaven?" The young man (from today's reading) thought he had it all figured out—he simply needed to do good things (16, 20). But Jesus challenged him with what it meant to be "good" (17). He then showed the man that just being good isn't good enough... To earn salvation, you must be perfect (21). By the end of the conversation Jesus made it clear there were two things preventing this man from gaining eternal life: (1) his attachment to wealth, and (2) his belief that salvation could be earned through good works. Jesus affirmed that there is only one to get to heaven: "Follow me" (21, 28). The man left sad. Thankfully we can learn from others' mistakes.

MEDITATE:

MATTHEW 19:26
Jesus looked at them and said, "With man this is impossible, but with God all things are possible."

97 BORN AGAIN

PRAY IT:
Jesus, thank You for loving me so much that You died for me. That truth is one that is shaping my life as a follower of You. I'm so grateful for Your love.

READ IT:
John 3:1-21

THINK ABOUT IT:
Is there anything about Nicodemus that surprises you? If so, what?

TRY IT:
Spend a few minutes talking to Jesus, imagining that he has personally addressed this challenge to you: "You must be born again…"

WRITE IT:
How would you explain being born again to someone who doesn't know much or anything about Jesus? Carefully think about it and write it out here.

In spite of Nicodemus's high position and religious knowledge (1, 10), he was not "born again" (3, 5). But what does it mean to be "born again"? Does it mean going to church/youth group? Does it mean doing good things? Even good things in the name of Jesus? Well, Jesus defined being "born again" as believing that he was the Son of God who died on the cross to save humanity from their sin (14-18). That was a lot for Nicodemus to consider. There's no evidence in today's reading that Nicodemus accepted Jesus' message. But later, Nicodemus did defend Jesus (see John 7:50-51) and he also publicly identified himself as a follower of Jesus (see John 19:38-42). No matter how it happens or how long it takes, the bottom line is: be born again.

MEDITATE:

JOHN 3:16-17
For God so loved the world that he gave his one and only Son, that whoever believes in him shall not perish but have eternal life. For God did not send his Son into the world to condemn the world, but to save the world through him.

98 NO MORE SHAME

PRAY IT:
Jesus, thank You for Your forgiveness, for Your love, for Your compassion. Thank You that You know everything about me and love me deeply. I'm blown away by Your love for me.

READ IT:
John 4:1-42

THINK ABOUT IT:
How would you feel if you met a stranger who knew all your worst secrets?

TRY IT:
Think deeply about the students who show up to youth group feeling shame. How do they usually act? What do they need the most? How might you (and/or your youth group) be able to meet their needs?

WRITE IT:
Make a list of 5 reasons why this story is good news. Make an attempt to share one of those reasons with a friend.

The woman in our passage today was carrying more than just a water jug as she walked to the well: her heart was burdened down with sin and shame. How do we know? She was a Samaritan, which is a race of people who were hated by the Jewish people (9). But, probably most significant was that her sinful lifestyle choices had produced a series of broken relationships (17-18). Thankfully, her sin and shame didn't keep Jesus away. Jesus graciously changed her life when he revealed he was the source of "living water" (10, 13-14). Then he told her that soon, all people could have a relationship with God because God's promised Messiah had arrived (23-24). This good news not only changed her life, but she went running to tell everyone the news (39-42). What a great response to a changed life.

MEDITATE:

JOHN 4:13-14
Jesus answered, "Everyone who drinks this water will be thirsty again, but whoever drinks the water I give them will never thirst. Indeed, the water I give them will become in them a spring of water welling up to eternal life."

99 LIFE-CHANGE

PRAY IT:

Jesus, thank You for changing my life! I was blind and now I see. I want my story to help others and bring them closer to You.

READ IT:

Acts 9:1-19

THINK ABOUT IT:

Reflect on your own spiritual story… What was the turning point or "Damascus Road" experience for you?

TRY IT:

Share your spiritual testimony with someone this week. You may need to write it out first.

WRITE IT:

Write out your personal story of life-change. No one can argue with your story—it's all yours. What were the main events that triggered your conversion? Recount those and begin crafting your testimony.

Saul was an angry young man (see Acts 7:58). He hated Christians and hunted them down to throw them into prison (verses 1-2). His eventual conversion changed everything! Saul literally "saw the light" and it burned away his anger. He went from wanting to kill Christians to preaching about Jesus. It's quite the story of life-change. Some people have radical conversion stories like Saul and some have testimonies that are not as dramatic, but equally life-changing. Some Christians will apologize and say, "My testimony is not that dramatic," as if the only way to be truly converted is to get knocked to the ground and hear the voice of Jesus. Regardless of your story, be thankful God changed you and you can share that story of life-change with others.

MEDITATE:

ACTS 9:4-5

He fell to the ground and heard a voice say to him, "Saul, Saul, why do you persecute me?" "Who are you, Lord?" Saul asked. "I am Jesus, whom you are persecuting," he replied.

100 I KNOW WHO YOU ARE

PRAY IT:

Jesus, this has been an amazing journey reading through Your Word! I have learned so much and am committed to drawing close to You and following Your ways. I'm so thankful for Your Word and Your commitment to love me as I continue to grow and learn.

READ IT:

Luke 9:18-27

THINK ABOUT IT:

How has your understanding of Jesus changed since you began reading this book?

TRY IT:

Spend a few minutes talking to Jesus as if he asked you this same question: "Who do *you* say that I am?"

WRITE IT:

Pick one of the following descriptions of Jesus (left-hand side) and then look up the verses connected. After reading the verses, write a short summary about how your understanding of Jesus has changed or been strengthened since you began reading this book.

He's the promised Messiah	(Psalm 110, 118)
He's the promised Savior	(Micah 5:1-5, Zechariah 12:1–13:9)
He's the divine son	(Matthew 3:17, 16:16)
He's the eternal God	(John 1:1-14, Colossians 1:15-20)
He's the sacrifice for our sin	(John 1:29, 1 Peter 1:24, Hebrews 9:28)
He's the way to life with God	(John 14:6)

MEDITATE:

LUKE 9:23-24

Then he said to them all: "Whoever wants to be my disciple must deny themselves and take up their cross daily and follow me. For whoever wants to save their life will lose it, but whoever loses their life for me will save it. What good is it for someone to gain the whole world, and yet lose or forfeit their very self?"

DISCUSSION QUESTIONS:
WHO IS JESUS… TO YOU?

PURPOSE:
To know how to be saved and have full confidence in Jesus.

QUESTIONS

1. Why do so many people believe that salvation can be earned by doing enough good deeds? Why would they struggle with the idea that salvation is a free gift from God?

2. Jesus said you cannot serve both God and money (Matthew 6:24). How can we know when we've crossed the line, that we love money and possessions too much?

3. For Nicodemus, coming to faith in Jesus was a process. Describe how you have discovered who Jesus is. How long has it taken and what do you think the next faith step might be?

4. The woman at the well struggled with her sense of shame. Have you ever felt like your past was holding you back from knowing God? What happened?

5. Early in his life, Saul was an angry person. Have you ever had a phase in your life when you were angry at God? Why? Were you able to resolve the source of your anger? How?

6. Peter boldly declared his belief in Jesus. Have you ever publicly explained what you believe about Jesus? What happened? Do you remember the first time you spoke up for Jesus?

7. Who is Jesus to you? Sum it up with just a few sentences.

CONGRATULATIONS! WAY TO GO!
YOU'VE COMPLETED THE ESSENTIAL JESUS!

You have prayed, read, and reflected on 100 essential passages about Jesus. That's a huge accomplishment, and you should celebrate. Really! That's a big deal and few are disciplined enough to complete the whole thing. We hope you share the good news with someone close to you.

But, the journey isn't over... We want to encourage you to keep growing in your faith, drawing closer to Jesus and becoming more like him. Continue to talk to Jesus daily through prayer, reading the Bible, and reflecting on what God's Word means for your life.

We have created another study much like this one; it's called *The Essential 100*. Now that you have a better understand of Jesus, you can grab an overview of the Bible and see God's amazing story unfold. In *The Essential 100*, you'll explore 100 of the most important passages from the Old Testament (50 readings) and from the New Testament (50 readings). If you enjoyed working through *The Essential Jesus*, you'll learn and grow with E100®.

AUTHOR BIOS

DOUG FIELDS

Doug Fields has a long history of youth ministry influence. First and foremost he has been a youth pastor for over 30 years at both Mariners and Saddleback Church in Southern California. He has been a speaker and trainer for Youth Specialties for 25 years, he founded Simply Youth Ministry (now owned by Group Publishing), and is the co-founder of Downloadyouthministry.com. A prolific author and co-author of over 60 books, Doug is thrilled to partner with Scripture Union and be part of *The Essential Jesus* and *The Essential 100* products. You can find more about Doug, his family, his books, and his ministry at www.dougfields.com.

WHITNEY T. KUNIHOLM

Whitney T. Kuniholm is the President of Scripture Union USA (ScriptureUnion.org), author of several books including *The Essential 100*, *The Essential Jesus,* and *The Essential Question*, and is a frequent contributor to Scripture Union's quarterly Bible reading guide, *Encounter with God*. He also has a blog (EssentialBibleBlog.com) and speaks at churches and Christian conferences.